# Disciples *of* Courage

## Ten Christian Lives that Inspire

Brendan Comerford SJ

ISBN 978 1 78812 567 3

Designed by Messenger Publications Design Department
Typeset in Adobe Garamond Pro & Cormorant Garamond
Printed by Hussar Books

Messenger Publications,
37 Leeson Place, Dublin D02 E5V0
www.messenger.ie

# CONTENTS

# PREFACE

The purpose of this short book is to introduce the reader to the lives of ten witnesses to Christian faith from very recent times. Each chapter has a similar pattern – following the life of each one from birth to death. The order of the chapters is dictated by the year of the death of each character, hence the book begins with Edith Stein (+1942) and ends with Roger of Taizé (+2005).

I stress that this book is merely an introduction. It had its origin in a series of six-day retreats that I gave, based on the lives, thought and witness of each one of these people.

The book is merely an introduction, so, while I givie direct quotations from each character, I do not provide footnotes or endnotes. At the end of the book there is a short bibliography for each chapter, which the reader may wish to consult.

The ten Christian disciples I deal with lived rich and varied lives. Three were converts to Roman Catholicism, one from Judaism. Two were Lutherans. Five are now canonised saints and the cause for the beatification of both Pedro Arrupe and Dorothy Day has already been introduced.

What attracted me to these ten people was the depth of their lived experience – unique to each one naturally but also with aspects in common: their journey to faith; the profundity of their prayer; their personal struggles with their own humanity; their experience of loneliness and fear; their courage; but pre-eminently their lived companionship with Jesus Christ.

May you, the reader, be enriched and inspired by these disciples of courage, and may you be helped by the short reflection from each one at the close of each chapter.

Brendan Comerford SJ

# CHAPTER ONE

# Edith Stein
## (1891–1942)

## Childhood

Edith Stein was born in Breslau, Germany (now Wroclaw, Poland) on 12 October 1891, the youngest of eleven children of a devout Jewish family. The day of her birth was the Jewish feast of Yom Kippur – the Day of Atonement. The Day of Atonement is described in the Old Testament Book of Leviticus. Once a year, the high priest would enter the Holy of Holies in the Temple in Jerusalem to offer sacrifice. Two of the sacrificial animals were goats; one of them (the 'scapegoat') was burdened with the people's sins and sent into the wilderness; the other was slaughtered and its blood shed on the Ark of the Covenant. Edith grew up thinking that Yom Kippur was, in some way, her special feast. Ironically, the witness of Edith's life and death has resonances with the meaning of the Day of Atonement. What is atonement? It is, quite literally in English, at-one-ment. It is the reconciliation between people and God. Edith would later see her Carmelite vocation as standing before God for all people.

As the youngest of the Stein siblings, Edith was surrounded from the first by a family of devoted grown-ups. Four of the Stein children had died in infancy. Only Erna, not quite two years Edith's senior, shared infancy with Edith. The rest of her sisters and brothers were no longer considered children, but had assumed the tasks and responsibilities of young adults.

Edith's father, Siegfried Stein, died at the age of forty-eight. Edith was not even two at the time. Auguste Stein, her mother, was left with the care of the children and the management of a debt-ridden lumber business. Frau Stein set off for the lumberyard at first light and the little ones did not see her until she returned home at the onset of dark. Taking a cue from their older siblings, Erna and Edith learned to keep the evening hours as restful for their mother as they could.

As a little girl, Edith remembered that she was always interrupting grown-ups' conversation and trying to impress them with her clever remarks. Somewhat like Thérèse of Lisieux (as a little child), Edith developed an unconscious vanity, and when she didn't reach her goal – to prove that she was the best and the smartest – she vented her frustration in tears of rage. At this early stage in Edith's life, she began to exhibit publicly the highest individual trait her family had noticed and remarked upon – she was absolutely dedicated to truth. She was intent on finding it and learning all about it. When she was sure of something – when she knew it to be true – she could not be budged from it by any means.

On her sixth birthday, Edith was received at mid-term at the Victoria School in Breslau. Her years at the Victoria School were devoted to soaking up every bit of knowledge that came her way. After seven years there, Edith was suddenly convinced that she had had enough of school. She informed the family that she was taking off for Hamburg to spend some time with her elder sister, Else. Frau Stein gave Edith her permission to take this unusual step.

Else was married to Dr Max Gordon and they had two children. Edith acted as housekeeper and nursemaid though, as we shall see later, one might wonder at her prowess as a housekeeper! In her free time, Edith took to reading the medical books and journals in Dr Gordon's library. Later she commented that, in Hamburg, she read many things not meant for a fifteen-year old girl!

Edith spent ten months in Hamburg. Her return to the maternal home was brought about by the critical illness of her baby nephew, Harald. He died within days of her return. Edith had become more introspective than before her Hamburg sojourn.

By the age of thirteen Edith had already begun to make an internal break with her family by consciously abandoning the practice of prayer. She acknowledged years later that from the age of thirteen to twenty-one she could not believe in the existence of a personal God. Her mother's complete absorption in God, however, did edify her.

In secondary school, the Obersekunda in Breslau, Edith plunged herself into the study of German literature, Latin and mathematics. Latin grammar, with its strict rules, fascinated her. She easily made up the year of school she had missed. With excellent marks, she continued her studies as preparation for attending the University of Breslau.

# The academic

On 27 April 1911, Edith entered the University of Breslau. She registered for the required courses in German and history but also attended lectures in psychology. She then came upon a book destined to revolutionise her intellectual life, *Logical Investigations*, by the philosopher Edmund Husserl (1859–1938). Edith moved to the University of Göttingen in Lower Saxony so that she could study under him. She was destined to spend many years here as his disciple. Husserl's belief was that philosophy practised as a rigorous science would lead to the discovery of truth. He trained his students to look at everything with strict impartiality and do away with their rationalist blinkers.

In Göttingen, Edith was introduced to the philosopher Max Ferdinand Scheler (1874–1928). Scheler was a Jewish convert to Roman Catholicism and, at the time Edith attended his lectures, he was filled with admiration for the spiritual beauty of Catholicism. Edith wrote of him: 'The brightness of a higher realm shone from his large blue eyes.'

One of the people whom Edith admired was the lecturer Adolf Reinach (1883–1917). He was Husserl's most valued colleague. He encouraged Edith when she was writing her doctoral thesis. Her mental struggles when writing her dissertations became excruciating and she admits she was unable to sleep and made little effort to eat sensibly; she sacrificed everything, apparently, to the absolute limits of her powers. During the First World War, while Reinach was serving in the German army, he and his wife were baptised as Lutherans. He wrote from the battlefield that in future his role as a philosopher was to bring others to faith.

When war was declared, Edith returned to Breslau in mid-semester. She was shocked that her relatives could speak of the war as something apart from themselves. She, on the other hand, felt herself to be so involved that only her joining the Red Cross nursing corps could satisfy her need to do something for her country.

At a military hospital in Austria, Edith cared for Austrian soldiers who were suffering from typhus, dysentery and cholera. She had her first experience of personally attending to the dying. Soldiers, far from their loved ones, dreaded being alone most of all. On completion of her service as a volunteer at a military hospital, Edith was awarded the medal of valour in recognition of her selfless service. When she returned to Göttingen, her landlady said of her: 'Fraülein Stein has seen much in this time; she has changed, too.'

In 1916, Husserl was offered a professorship at the University of Freiburg. He asked Edith to accompany him as his graduate assistant. During her first summer there, she submitted her thesis on *The Problem of Empathy* and was awarded the doctoral degree *summa cum laude* (with the highest praise) on 3 August 1916. In this thesis, Edith examined empathy ('the power of identifying oneself mentally with [and so fully comprehending] a person or object of contemplation' – *Concise Oxford Dictionary*) as a particular way of knowing – she wrote chapters on empathy in its social, ethical and aesthetic dimensions. What interested Edith most was the question of defining the possibility of mutual communication between human beings, in other words, the possibility of establishing community.

## Journey of faith

In 1917, Edith received the very painful news that Adolf Reinach had been killed on the battlefields of Flanders. She felt totally disoriented by his death. She wondered how she would ever be able to find the words to say to the grieving widow, Anna.

The resignation Edith encountered when she met Frau Reinach struck her like a ray from a hidden world. Rather than appearing crushed by her suffering, the young widow, Anna, was filled with a hope that offered the other mourners consolation and peace. Edith's rational approach to life crumbled in the face of this experience. The light of faith broke in upon her – in the mystery of the Cross. Shortly before her own death, Edith told a Jesuit friend: 'It was the first encounter with the Cross and the divine power that it bestows on those who carry it. For the first time, I was seeing with my very eyes the Church, born from her Redeemer's sufferings, triumphant over the sting of death. That was the moment my unbelief collapsed and Christ shone forth – in the mystery of the Cross.'

Edith began to read the New Testament, wondering whether she would eventually convert to Lutheranism or Catholicism. As she came closer to faith, she began to experience a sense of 'resting in God' and an inner yearning for Christ. Formerly unnoticed 'coincidences' of daily life suddenly took on the aspects of God's loving providence.

One day, Edith happened to be in Frankfurt with some friends and they decided to visit the Roman Catholic cathedral. What happened next affected Edith deeply:

We went into the cathedral for a few minutes, and as we stood there in respectful silence, a woman came in with her shopping basket and knelt down in one of the pews to say a short prayer. That was something completely new to me. In the synagogue, as in the Protestant churches I had visited, people only went in at the time of service. But here was someone coming into an empty church in the middle of a day's work as if to talk to a friend. I have never been able to forget that.

A simple occurrence for us, perhaps, one we have seen so often, but look at the effect it had on Edith.

One evening in the summer of 1921, Edith was staying with some friends, Hans-Theodor and Hedwig Conrad. Her hosts had gone out for the evening; she was in the house alone. She went in search of something to read. By chance, her eyes fell on St Teresa of Avila's autobiography. Once Edith began reading it, she found it impossible to put the book down and stayed up reading the entire night. When she finally finished reading it the next morning, she said to herself, 'This is truth!'

What Edith found in Teresa's autobiography was the confirmation of her own experience. God is not a God of knowledge, God is love. God does not reveal God's mysteries to the deductive intelligence, but to the heart that surrenders itself to God.

Edith was baptised a Roman Catholic on 1 January 1922, taking the name 'Teresa' as her baptismal name. She was thirty-one years old when she was baptised and received the Eucharist for the first time. A short time later, she received Confirmation from the Bishop of Speyer. Together with the faith had come the interior call to consecrate herself to God by becoming a Carmelite nun. She kept this resolution to herself, sharing it only with her spiritual director, Canon Joseph Schwind. He advised her to hasten slowly. Religious orders had an unwritten custom of requiring an interval of at least three years between adult baptism and entrance into religious life.

Edith's mothers's reaction to Edith's conversion caught her unawares – Frau Stein wept. Edith had never seen her mother cry before. She continued to attend synagogue with her mother, surprising her by praying the psalms of the synagogue out of the Roman breviary (prayer book).

Edith had been disappointed, but not surprised, by the treatment she had received from the all-male Göttingen faculty when she sought a professorship in the autumn of 1920. Her work with Husserl had coincided with the years of the First World War, and when the men returned to the university setting, jealousy of her work was evident. Her rejection by the university's board (they returned her application for the professorship and her thesis without even reading it) caused Edith mental and physical distress. She gave up plans for a scholarly career and accepted a position teaching German at Saint Magdalena's, the Dominican school for girls in Speyer, at Canon Schwind's suggestion. She was to spend the next eight years at Saint Magdalena's.

In 1925, Edith was introduced to the Jesuit priest and philosopher of religion, Erich Przywara (1889–1972). He spoke of Edith's great effectiveness as a teacher and of her formative influence on her students. He asked Edith to translate into German some of the letters of Cardinal John Henry Newman. This was the beginning of a lively intellectual relationship between Edith and Przywara. Edith expressed an interest in taking on other projects. Przywara recommended that she translate some of Thomas Aquinas's work. The work he suggested was *Disputed Questions on Truth*. As Edith worked on this translation she said: 'I have gradually come to the realisation that ... the deeper one is drawn into God, the more he needs to go out of himself – out into the world, that is, to carry the divine life into it.'

It was also Erich Przywara who urged Edith (at the time when Hitler was beginning to reveal the perverted plan he meant to pursue), to write about life in a Jewish family, and so we have today *Life in a Jewish family 1891–1916*. Edith got only so far in her story.

Edith had adopted the practice of praying at night, often spending whole nights by herself in the convent chapel. In the morning she would go to teach as if nothing extraordinary were happening. She lived like a Dominican among Dominicans, refusing to take any salary beyond what was necessary for food, clothing and board.

Already in 1930, when Edith was becoming impatient to lead the life of a Carmelite, she wrote of the necessity of her own *holocaustum* (holocaust). She used the Latin form as it appeared in the breviary. Thérèse of Lisieux also chose this term – she spoke of herself as '*victime d'holocauste*'. The word comes from two Greek words: *holos*, meaning 'whole' and *kaustus*, meaning 'burnt'. It was to prove so prophetically accurate in Edith's case.

During the school holidays, Edith lectured in many cities in Germany, Austria and Switzerland to large audiences of educators and professional women's societies. Her strong sense of social responsibility led her to an active participation in the struggle for women's suffrage. There was also another central idea she sought to develop: woman's Christian life as a source of healing for the world. Her lecture titles indicate the issues they treated: 'The Ethos of Woman's Vocation'; 'The Life of the Christian Woman'; 'Foundations of Woman's Vocation'; 'The Place of Women in Guiding the Young to the Church'. Edith held that every woman should try to find 'breathing spaces' – moments in which she can return to herself and rest in God.

Edith left Saint Magdalena's in March 1931 in order to devote herself to full-time writing. Most of 1931 was spent unsuccessfully applying to the universities of Freiburg and Breslau. Anti-semitism was at work behind the scenes to obstruct the appointment. Just at this time, however, an offer did arrive from the German Institute for Scientific Pedagogy in Münster. Edith took the post. She lived at the Collegium Marianum, a house of studies for young religious in Münster. Sometimes, in the midst of her busy schedule, she would yearn to go apart for a while and celebrate her 'silent liturgy' (her name for private prayer) or share in the fullness of the divine praise at the Benedictine Archabbey of Beuron (near Baden Württemberg) where the abbot, Raphael Waltzer, was her spiritual director.

Two years later, in 1933, Edith looked on horrified as university students began violently attacking Jews. She worried intensely about her family and friends in Breslau. At the time, Edith's own position as a Catholic at a Catholic Institute seemed relatively secure.

At Easter 1933, while travelling to Beuron to consult with Abbot Walter, Edith interrupted her journey to attend Holy Hour at the Carmelite convent in Cologne. During the service, she found her thoughts wandering from the homilist's words:

> I spoke with the Saviour to tell him that it was his Cross that was now being laid on the Jewish people, that the few who understood this had the responsibility of carrying it in the name of all, and that I myself was willing to do this, if he would only show me how. I left the service with the inner conviction that I had been heard, but uncertain as ever as to what 'carrying the Cross' would mean for me.

Edith felt called to take action on behalf of her people. She submitted a request for a private papal audience with Pope Pius XI, hoping that a special encyclical would alleviate the situation of the Jewish people. When she returned to Münster from Beuron, she learned that her request for a papal audience had been refused. She sent her appeal in writing to Pius XI, who responded with a blessing for herself and her family. Edith realised that most people could not grasp the urgency of the threat as she did. Her alarm proved personally wholly justified – scarcely had she returned to Münster when she was told that she would have to relinquish her teaching position. Hitler had passed a law forbidding Jews to teach or to work in any of the civil service professions. Edith realised that she would never be able to work in Germany again.

Edith was offered a teaching post in South America but, after giving the matter careful consideration, she was now convinced that the time had come for fulfilling her hopes to enter the Carmelite convent in Cologne. She worried that she might be too old to be accepted (she was forty-two), but the nuns were impressed with her, and in mid-June 1933, they notified her of her acceptance.

## The Carmel in Cologne

On 1 September 1933, Edith told her mother of her intention to enter Carmel. From that moment a cloud hung over the entire house, as her family tried to shake her resolution. In despair her mother cried out:

> I don't want to say anything against him. He may have been a very good man. But why did he make himself God?

One relative said to Edith that she had embraced 'the religion of our persecutors'. The family opposition continued. Edith wrote later:

> In my immediate surroundings, I saw only the very great pain, in the face of which my leaving appeared to be an unspeakable cruelty. Time and time again, I asked myself during those weeks, 'Which of us is going to break first – me or my mother? But the two of us held out to the very last day.

Edith's last day at home was her birthday, 12 October. She went to the synagogue with her mother for the last time. She entered the Carmel in Cologne on 13 October 1933. Because her mother regarded Edith's reception of the Carmelite habit as the ultimate break between her daughter and the Jewish people, not only did she not attend Edith's clothing ceremony, but in the following years she refused to answer any of the weekly letters Edith mailed from Cologne.

Edith's clothing ceremony took place on 15 April 1934. On this day, she received the Carmelite habit, and her new name, Teresa Benedicta of the

Cross. Known as Sister Benedicta – the name taken out of gratitude to Beuron Archabbey – she was flanked by two symbolic titles: Teresa, representing her conversion and call to prayer; and the Cross, which Edith would carry in Carmel and beyond. Edith asked for the title, 'a Cruce', 'of the Cross', because of her belief that suffering in this life, of whatever nature, can be united to the suffering of Christ on the Cross. Many friends and former colleagues came to the clothing ceremony. Edmund Husserl sent a telegram. None of Edith's brothers or sisters attended the clothing ceremony, though some did send congratulations.

During the two years of her novitiate (initial religious formation), Edith said that she never laughed so much! However, all was not laughter. Edith gradually returned to writing, in accordance with her superior's wishes. She completed the index of her translation of Thomas Aquinas and contributed to a number of periodicals. Edith wrote of her meditations at this time:

> Think of me in the old brown habit and close to the ground as ever. It's the same with my meditations. They're not any great, soaring spiritual flights, but very simple and down to earth. Their main value is that they express my gratitude at having this place as my earthly home.

Edith pronounced her simple vows of poverty, chastity and obedience on Easter Sunday, 1935. The first major task she was given as a simply professed nun came in the form of a commission from her superiors to finish the manuscript of *Act and Potency*, a work she had begun at Saint Magdalena's in Speyer. Edith appreciated the foresight shown by her superiors in allowing her to continue with philosophical research within the boundaries of her vocation. Mother Renata, her Mistress of Novices, valued Edith's gifts as a scholar and philosopher.

Edith completed her study in the summer of 1936. While waiting for an answer from the publishers to whom she had submitted the work (now entitled *Finite and Eternal Being*), she received the news of her mother's death. Frau Stein had died in Breslau on 14 September 1936, the Feast of the Holy Cross, after a long and painful struggle. She died unreconciled to Edith's decision. Ironically, the winter following Frau Stein's death, Edith had the joy of seeing her sister, Rosa, enter the Roman Catholic Church.

When it came to housework in the convent, Edith was always making all kinds of mistakes on account of her lack of practical experience. She wrote to a friend:

One thing is certain: it has been good training in humility for me that I'm regularly given tasks where all my efforts produce such unsatisfactory results.

In housework, Edith had to concede defeat! Totally unaccustomed to it, she swept the floor as if she were pulling a dog along by the collar. Asked to do some sewing, she handed in the finished work with colossal stitches, all of them crooked. She accepted all her mistakes with a good-humoured smile.

Edith made her final profession on 1 May 1938. Auxiliary Bishop Wilhelm Stockums of Cologne received her vows. The symbol of her final commitment was the black veil of the professed Carmelite nun.

Outside the convent walls came the terrible SS attack of 8 November 1938 – *Kristallnacht* – when Jewish citizens were driven from their homes with clubs, and their businesses demolished or confiscated. In a matter of hours, their lives as members of German society had been destroyed. Even the synagogues had been burned. There was no public outcry against the violence. Very quickly the German people had learned that any such protest would be ruthlessly and immediately suppressed.

## The Carmel in Echt

The Prioress of the Cologne Carmel decided to have Edith transferred to the Dutch convent of Echt, founded by nuns from Cologne There were seventeen nuns in the convent there, fourteen of whom were German. Edith left Cologne on 31 December 1938.

In 1940, Edith was able to welcome her sister, Rosa, to the Carmel in Echt – Rosa had managed to escape through Belgium. She acted as extern help to the community along with another laywoman. However, on 10 May 1940, the Netherlands was invaded by the Nazis. Edith and Rosa had to present themselves to the Gestapo and the SS at Maastricht to fill out numerous forms, giving their personal details and whereabouts.

In the convent it was evident to the sisters that Edith was a person of deep and continual prayer. During air raids, for example, while many sisters were shaking with fear, Edith was noticeably motionless, sitting in prayer. She never tried to *sound* holy. She avoided the topic of her prayer and said nothing about her interior life. Instead, she spoke about things that would amuse, such as a story about the Jesuits of Cologne who doctored a statue of St John of the Cross until it became St Ignatius Loyola! In the early mornings in chapel, Edith would often fall asleep while sitting on the floor, resting on her heels. Other sisters would wake her with a nudge; she would smile at them and go back to sleep!

Meanwhile, Edith's prioress had asked her to write a book on St John of the Cross in preparation for the fourth centenary of his birth in Spain, 24 June 1542. This was to be *The Science of the Cross*, the last of Edith's writings.

Edith hoped that she could escape with Rosa to a Carmel in Switzerland but the convent there said that there was accommodation only for Edith and she refused to leave without Rosa. The final week of July 1942 brought the whole question of finding refuge in Switzerland to the fore again. A letter from Mother Marie Agnes, from the monastery of Le Paquier, contained the long-awaited confirmation that Rosa, too, would find shelter with the Third Order Carmelites, whose convent was an hour's drive from the Swiss monastery.

On 26 July 1942, the fateful pastoral letter of the Dutch hierarchy, condemning the Nazi persecution of the Jews, was read aloud in the parish churches of the Netherlands. The SS would take revenge on all priests and nuns who were Jewish by birth. On the very same day, the Superior General of the Discalced Carmelites, Fr Peter Thomas, arrived in Echt. He specifically asked Edith what her personal preferences were regarding a permanent transfer and what she would like to do. She told him she would most like to remain right where she was, in Echt.

Edith received word on 28 July 1942, that her brother Paul, his wife Trude, and their sister Frieda had all been arrested and sent to Theresienstadt (in the German-occupied region of the then Czechoslovakia). There, they too would die as victims of the Nazis within a year of Edith's and Rosa's deaths.

## Final days

Ironically, on 2 August, Edith had just finished her description of the death of St John of the Cross. On the same day the SS arrested Edith, along with many other Catholic Jews, in retaliation for the Catholic bishops' pastoral letter of protest against the persecution of the Jews which had been publicly read in all churches the previous month. The Prioress of Echt Carmel was summoned to the parlour by two SS officers and ordered to produce Edith. By the time Edith reached the convent gate under guard, Rosa was already there. To the terrified Rosa, Edith said, 'Come, Rosa, let us go for our people.' They were herded into a police van and driven away to the detention camp of Westerbork in North Holland.

Edith and Rosa, with 1,200 other prisoners, spent three days in Westerbork. Witnesses to these events and to Edith's attitude in the concentration camp speak of her complete calm and self-possession. Edith immediately set about taking care of the children. She washed them, combed their hair, and tried to make sure they were fed and cared for. One witness said that every time she thought of Edith sitting in the barracks, the same picture came to mind: 'a Pietà without the Christ'.

When Edith and Rosa were arrested, Edith's breviary (prayerbook) was among the few articles she managed to take with her. On 6 August, in her final letter from Barrack 36 to Mother Ambrosia at Echt, Edith tells her prioress, 'so far I have been able to pray, gloriously'.

On 7 August 1942, thousands of men, women and children were herded into sealed cattle trucks, bound for Auschwitz. A report of Edith's arrest and imprisonment appeared in the Vatican newspaper, *Osservatore Romano*, in 1947. It is generally accepted that she was executed in the gas chambers of Auschwitz on 9 August 1942. Only in 1958, through the International Red Cross in Holland, was final certification of the deaths of Edith and Rosa received.

On 1 May 1987, Edith Stein was beatified by Pope John Paul II in a ceremony attended by more than 70,000 people in Cologne's largest stadium. She was canonised by John Paul II on 11 October 1998 and later declared Co-Patroness of Europe, along with Saints Benedict, Cyril and Methodius, Bridget of Sweden and Catherine of Siena.

Edith Stein's feast day is 9 August, in memory of the likely date of her death, of her being born into Life Eternal.

## Reflection

Each day I take whatever comes and pray only that the necessary abilities be given me for whatever is required of me. In any case, it is a prime school of humility when you constantly find the things it is your duty to do are accomplished in a very imperfect manner, despite your having completed them with such great effort.

# CHAPTER TWO

# Dietrich Bonhoeffer

(1906–1945)

## Childhood

Dietrich Bonhoeffer was born into a privileged, cultured and prestigious family in the same city as Edith Stein – Breslau, Germany (now Wroclaw, Poland) on 4 February 1906. He was a twin, his sister, Sabine, being born ten minutes later. He was one of eight children. His father, Dr Karl Bonhoeffer, was a distinguished university professor and physician. From 1904 to 1912 he was professor of psychiatry and neurology in Breslau University. In 1912, he was appointed professor of the same disciplines at the University of Berlin. Professor Bonhoeffer's family is readily traced back to the sixteenth century and included doctors, clergy, lawyers and burgomasters among its members.

Dietrich's mother's family heritage is likewise notable. His maternal great-grandfather was Karl August von Hase (1800–1890) who earned a widespread reputation as a church historian at the University of Jena. His grandfather was Karl Alfred von Hase (1842–1914), who for several years served as Court Preacher to Wilhelm II, the last of the Hohenzollern emperors in Germany. Karl Alfred von Hase was also a distinguished professor of theology in Breslau.

Paula von Hase Bonhoeffer, Dietrich's mother, was completely devoted to her large family. In Berlin, she presided over a staff of seven. She taught the older children at home.

The Bonhoeffers did not attend weekly worship in the neighbourhood church but Paula, the mother, was consistently concerned that the children encounter stories from the Bible, learn the great hymns of the Christian tradition, offer grace before meals, participate in evening prayers, and be baptised and confirmed in the faith.

Family life was also shaped by holidays spent at a second home in Friedrichsbrunn in the eastern Harz Mountains. This provided occasions for experiencing the natural joys of hills and forests, of swimming, hiking, singing folk songs and reading. That this segment of family life made its indelible impression on Dietrich's own life is evidenced in the fact that he recalls Friedrichsbrunn no fewer than six times in his prison letters.

At the age of seven, Dietrich went to the Friedrich Werner grammar school. He cultivated his musical skills and, at ten, he was playing Mozart sonatas. He got used at an early age to playing the piano in company without shyness or embarrassment. It was music that gave him a special position at school among his fellow students.

The serenity of the family was demonstrably shaken in the closing weeks of the First World War. Dietrich's brother, Walter, serving in the German army, was wounded on 23 April 1918, and died five days later. The effect on the parents was devastating. Paula Bonhoeffer withdrew from family life for weeks on end. Dietrich, only twelve years old at the time, was distraught. The parents gave Dietrich Walter's Confirmation bible, which he kept for the rest of his life.

While his older brothers were oriented towards the sciences, following the model of their empirically minded father, Dietrich's interests lay elsewhere. During his adolescent years, he read philosophy and religion, including such notables as Euripides (c.484–406 BC); Friedrich Schleiermacher (1768–1834); Johann Wolfgang von Goethe (1749–1832); Friedrich Schiller (1759–1805) and Max Weber (1864–1920).

Dietrich surprised and even somewhat dismayed his parents when he decided, at the age of fourteen, to become a theologian and later a pastor. When his older brother, Karl Friedrich, told him not to waste his life in such a 'poor, feeble, boring, bourgeois institution as the church,' Dietrich replied, 'If what you say is true, I shall reform it.'

## University days

At the age of seventeen, Dietrich entered Tübingen University, where his father and older brothers had also studied. His more informal education continued with a three-month visit to Rome, accompanied by his brother, Klaus. Holy Week 1924 in St Peter's made a powerful impact on him. Following their stay in Rome, Dietrich and Klaus continued their travels across the Mediterranean, spending several days in Sicily, Tripoli and the Libyan desert.

Later in 1924 Dietrich returned to his formal education at the University of Berlin, where he concentrated on his studies in theology for the next three years. His encounter there with some eminent theologians of the day was strategic in shaping his theological journey. His doctoral dissertation, *Sanctorum Communio* (Communion of Saints), in which he describes Christ as existing for community, was published in 1927.

Dietrich served for a year in a German Lutheran parish in Barcelona, Spain (1928–29). He was disappointed to discover that there was no real intellectual discussion in Spanish church circles. Still too young to be ordained, Dietrich went to the US in 1930 for postgraduate study and a teaching fellowship at New York's Union Theological Seminary. He was described by the theologian Reinhold Niebuhr as 'a brilliant and theologically sophisticated young man'. Niebuhr, one of his mentors, challenged him to think deeply about the church's involvement in the aches and pains of society.

Dietrich became acquainted with the poor district of Harlem in New York and, as he said himself, 'he began to see things from below' – from the perspective of those who suffer oppression. He attended the Abyssinian Baptist Church and observed, 'Here (in Harlem) one can truly speak and hear about sin and grace and the love of God … the Black Christ is preached with rapturous passion and vision.' He travelled by car through the US to Mexico, where he was invited to speak on the subject of peace at a public meeting arranged by a Quaker friend. His early visits to Italy, Libya, Spain, the US, Mexico and Cuba opened him to a more ecumenical viewpoint.

Bonhoeffer returned to Germany in 1931 and became a lecturer in theology in the University of Berlin. At this time he seems to have undergone something of a personal conversion from a theologian attracted to the intellectual side of Christianity to a dedicated man of faith, resolved to carry out the teaching of Christ as he found it revealed in the Gospels.

On 15 November 1931, at the age of twenty-five, Bonhoeffer was finally ordained at the old Prussian United Saint Matthew Church in Berlin. In addition to his academic work, he now served as a chaplain to a Technical University in Berlin and then became the teacher of a Confirmation class of fifty boys in a squalid and poverty-stricken area. On a number of occasions he preached at the prestigious Kaiser Wilhelm Memorial Church in Berlin and in other congregations. To Bonhoeffer, nothing in his calling competed in importance with preaching.

# The Nazis come to power

Bonhoeffer's promising academic and ecclesiastical career was dramatically altered when the Nazis came to power on 30 January 1933. He was a determined opponent of the Nazi regime from its first days. Two days after Hitler was installed as Chancellor, Bonhoeffer delivered a radio address in which he attacked Hitler and warned Germany against slipping into an idolatrous cult of the *Führer* (leader), who could well turn out to be *Verführer* (mis-leader or seducer), and was cut off in mid-sentence. In April 1933, Bonhoeffer raised the first voice for church resistance to Hitler's persecution of the Jews, declaring that the church must not simply 'bandage the victims under the wheel, but jam the spoke in the wheel itself'.

In July 1933, Hitler imposed new church elections of pastors and synods within the Protestant established churches. Hitler had said, 'German pastors are insignificant little people, submissive as dogs, you can do what you like with them.' Bonhoeffer put all his efforts into the election, campaigning for the selection of independent non-Nazi officials. The election, of course, was rigged, and an overwhelming majority of key positions went to Nazi-supported German Christians. There was the establishment of the Reichskirche under Ludwig Müller. All pastors of the Reichskirche had to swear an oath of service to Hitler. These 'German Christians' stated that the Old Testament must go, that Jesus was a non-Jew and an anti-Semite!

Disheartened by the German churches' complacency with the Nazi regime, in the autumn of 1933 the twenty-seven-year-old Bonhoeffer accepted a two-year appointment as a pastor of two German-speaking churches in London: the German Reformed Church of St Paul at Whitechapel and the German Evangelical Church in Sydenham. While in London, he tried to explain to his British friends, among them especially the Bishop of Chichester, Bishop George Bell, the true character of the German church struggle.

Bonhoeffer quickly realised that in the situation in which the world and the churches found themselves in the 1930s nothing would be gained any longer for these churches by simply citing their old creedal statements. The ecumenical movement seemed to him to offer the only way of uniting the various members of the body of Christ. Bonhoeffer considered it the duty of the churches to listen anew to the message of the Bible and to put themselves in the context of the whole Church. More than any other teacher in a German university or theological seminary, Bonhoeffer made German students familiar with the life, history and development of the non-Lutheran churches.

In 1934, Pastor Martin Niemöller, a friend of Bonhoeffer's, had formed the Confessing Church, a source of Christian opposition to the Nazi government. The Confessing Church insisted that Christ, not the Führer, was the head of the Church. In 1935, Bonhoeffer decided to return to Germany from England in order to become the director of an underground seminary for training Confessing Church pastors in Finkenwalde, near Stettin, Prussia. In this seminary an attempt was made to live a community life according to Christian standards – in brotherly love. It was to be a communal life in which Jesus Christ's call to discipleship was taken seriously. Bonhoeffer put his thoughts together on this subject in a small, deeply rich book entitled *Life Together*. Written in 1938 at his sister Sabine's home in Göttingen in only four weeks, it brought together the basic components of the seminarians' experience – personal and corporate meditation, prayer, solitude, Bible study, fellowship, recreation, ministry, worship, the Eucharist, confession and spiritual care.

In August 1936, Bonhoeffer's authorisation to teach at the University of Berlin was revoked after he was denounced as a pacifist and enemy of the state. By August 1937, Heinrich Himmler had decreed the education and examination of the Confessing Church ministry candidates illegal. In September 1937, the Gestapo closed the seminary at Finkenwalde and, by November, had arrested twenty-seven pastors and former students. It was around this time that Bonhoeffer published his best-known book, *The Cost of Discipleship*, a study of the Sermon on the Mount, in which he famously attacked 'cheap grace' as a cover for ethical laxity, but he also preached 'costly grace'. 'Cheap grace' is when the demands of God are silenced by trading on God's kindness. 'Costly grace' changes the Christian disciple from the inside out – it involves suffering because it involves following Christ. Christ's message of grace is 'I have loved you from eternity. Stay with me and you will live.'

In 1938, the Gestapo banned Bonhoeffer from Berlin. In February 1938, he had made an initial contact with members of the German Resistance, the Abwehr, when his brother-in-law, Hans von Dohnanyi, introduced him to a group seeking Hitler's overthrow. As the 1930s drew to a close, Bonhoeffer became increasingly disappointed and disillusioned about the Confessing Church's lack of forthrightness and assertiveness in the struggle against Nazism. Then there was the infamous Kristallnacht on 9 November 1938, when Nazi depravity destroyed more than 7,000 Jewish shops, burnt synagogues, desecrated Torah scrolls, murdered over ninety Jews and sent more than 20,000 to concentration camps.

By this stage, Bonhoeffer knew that war was imminent and he was troubled at the prospect of being conscripted. As a committed pacifist, opposed to the Nazi regime, he could never swear an oath to Hitler and fight in his army, although failure to do so was a capital offence.

Bonhoeffer left for the US in June 1939 at the invitation of the Union Theological Seminary in New York. He crossed the Atlantic with his brother, Karl Friedrich, who had been offered a professorship at the University of Chicago. Bonhoeffer was to travel on a lecture tour himself, plans having been laid enthusiastically by Reinhold Niebuhr, his friend and teacher from Union Seminary days. He was also to teach a summer course at Union, and undertake pastoral services to German refugees. None of those plans were to be fulfilled.

No sooner had Bonhoeffer arrived in the US than he regretted his decision in coming at all, despite strong pressure from his friends to stay. In a deeply moving letter to Reinhold Niebuhr, he etched his thoughts:

> I have come to the conclusion that I made a mistake in coming to America. I must live through this difficult period in our national history with the people of Germany. I will have no right to participate in the reconstruction of Christian life in Germany after the war if I do not share the trials of this time with my people ... Christians in Germany will have to face the terrible alternative of either willing the defeat of their nation in order that Christian civilization will survive, or willing the victory of their nation and thereby destroying civilization. I know which of these alternatives I must choose but I cannot make that choice from security.

After only twenty-six days in New York, Bonhoeffer returned to Germany on the last scheduled steamer to cross the Atlantic.

Back in Germany, Bonhoeffer was forbidden to speak in public and was required to report his activities to the police regularly. In 1941, he was forbidden to print or to publish. Convinced that true patriotism called for a concerted attempt to remove Hitler and his entourage from national leadership, Bonhoeffer became a civilian member of the Abwehr until his arrest on 9 April 1943.

Bonhoeffer presumably knew about various 1943 plots against Hitler through Hans von Doynanyi, who was actively involved in the planning.

Bonhoeffer did not justify his action but accepted that he was taking guilt upon himself when he wrote in his work *Ethics*:

> When a man takes guilt upon himself in responsibility, he imputes his guilt to himself and to no one else ... He answers for it ... Before other men he is justified by dire necessity; before himself he is acquitted by his conscience, but before God he hopes only for grace.

In *The Cost of Discipleship* Bonhoeffer had written:

> It is not only my task to look after the victims of madmen who drive a motor-car in a crowded street, but to do all in my power to stop their driving at all.

Arrangements were made to secure Bonhoeffer's exemption from the military draft, by insisting that his efforts were indispensable for espionage activities. The argument that finally persuaded a sceptical Gestapo was that Bonhoeffer's ecumenical contacts could be exceedingly useful for gathering intelligence information. Ostensibly, he could provide background for assessing the political situation in Allied as well as neutral countries. Of course, in his guise as a 'double agent', Bonhoeffer used his travels abroad as occasions to cultivate a closer communication between the Resistance and the Allies.

Bonhoeffer was instrumental in the implementation of a top-secret plan to assist in the smuggling of Jews out of Germany, referred to as 'Operation 7'. Three times he crossed the border to Switzerland, connecting with key ecumenical figures. He also travelled to Norway, making contacts for the Resistance. His encouragement strengthened the Norwegian Lutheran Church, its clergy and its leaders in their struggle against the Nazi occupiers of their country.

In May 1942, Bonhoeffer met his British ecumenical friend, Bishop George Bell, in Sigtuna, Sweden. In a secret rendezvous, Bonhoeffer relayed to the bishop precise information about the German resistance to Hitler, including names of key members of the underground. He also asked Bell to pass on an urgent message to British Foreign Secretary Anthony Eden, thence to Winston Churchill, as well as to President Franklin Roosevelt, requesting support for the Resistance and especially for negotiating a compromise peace after Hitler had been overthrown. There was no return message from the Allied leaders.

# Bonhoeffer in love

It was in Finkenwalde (where the seminary for the Confessing Church students was situated) that Bonhoeffer first met his future fiancée, Maria von Wedemeyer, the granddaughter of Ruth von Kleist-Retzow, who was a strong supporter of the Confessing Church and seminary. Numerous times in the late 1930s Bonhoeffer visited the von Kleist home, primarily at holiday times. It was there that he completed his manuscript of *The Cost of Discipleship* in 1937, and later worked on his *Ethics*. It was there, too, that he filled a pastoral role, particularly after Maria's father had been killed at Stalingrad and, a few months later, her brother Max. Right up to 1942, Dietrich was addressed by Maria's family as 'Pastor Bonhoeffer'.

Love blossomed that same year, even though Maria was just eighteen and Dietrich was already thirty-six. They became engaged on 13 January. Maria wrote in her letter of acceptance: 'With all my heart, I can now say yes.' The salutation of this monumental letter was still 'Dear Pastor Bonhoeffer!'

# Prison

Just a few weeks later, on 5 April 1943, the Gestapo arrested Bonhoeffer, his sister, Christel, and her husband, Hans von Dohnanyi, in the house of his parents. The Gestapo had searched von Dohnanyi's office and discovered notes revealing Bonhoeffer's foreign contacts and other documents related to the anti-Hitler conspiracy.

For a year and a half, Bonhoeffer was imprisoned in Berlin's Tegel military prison. In prison, he greatly inspired all those who came in contact with him by his indomitable courage, his unselfishness and his goodness. Sympathetic guards helped smuggle his letters out of cell 92 to reach the hands of Dietrich's parents, as well as Maria, and his theologian friend, Eberhard Bethge, then in the German army. These uncensored letters were posthumously published in *Letters and Papers from Prison*. Bonhoeffer was generally treated well in Tegel, perhaps because his uncle was a military commandant in Berlin. One of the guards, Corporal Knoboch, even offered to help Bonhoeffer escape from prison and 'disappear' with him, and plans were made to that end. But Bonhoeffer declined the offer, fearing Nazi retribution on his family.

Bonhoeffer's intellectual life while he was in prison was steadily stimulated by books on philosophy, poetry, music and theology that were brought by his parents, many upon his request.

In October 1944, after eighteen months in Tegel Prison, Bonhoeffer was transferred to the notorious Gestapo prison at Prinz-Albrecht-Strasse. By then the Gestapo, after relentless pursuit, had discovered secret papers and documents of the Abwehr in Zossen. The evidence was damning enough to incriminate key figures in the resistance and conspiracy, including Bonhoeffer and von Dohnanyi.

From February until April 1945, Bonhoeffer was an inmate of the concentration camp at Buchenwald. A British Secret Service inmate, a Captain Payne Best, was a fellow prisoner. He wrote of Bonhoeffer:

> He always seemed to diffuse an atmosphere of happiness, of joy in every smallest event in life, and a deep gratitude for the mere fact that he was alive ... He was one of the very few men I have ever met to whom his God was real and ever close to him.

Payne Best and Bonhoeffer were among 'special prisoners' who were loaded into a prison van heading for the extermination camp at Flossenbürg.

On 8 April 1945, Bonhoeffer was convicted of high treason and condemned to death by an SS judge at a court martial without witnesses or being allowed to speak in his own defence. He was executed in the grey dawn of 9 April, just two weeks before soldiers of the US 90th and 97th Infantry Division liberated the camp, a month before the surrender of Germany.

The camp doctor who witnessed the execution wrote:

> I saw Pastor Bonhoeffer ... kneeling on the floor praying fervently to God. I was most deeply moved by this lovable man, so devout and so certain that God heard his prayer. At the place of execution, he again said a short prayer and then climbed the few steps to the gallows, brave and composed. His death ensued after a few seconds. In the almost fifty years that I worked as a doctor, I have hardly ever seen a man die so entirely submissive to the will of God.

## Letters and papers from prison

Bonhoeffer's letters from Tegel prison to his parents, to Maria and especially to his theologian friend, Eberhard Bethge, date from April 1943 to December 1944. They appeared for the first time in 1950–51, edited by

Bethge. By the time a new English translation appeared in 1970, the book had been included among the 'religious classics'. The papers from prison include some poems, the outline of a possible book and miscellaneous thoughts.

Initially, in the letters to his parents, one gets the impression that Bonhoeffer wants to prevent them from being too anxious about his welfare in prison. The tone of the letters is sensitive, very human and, at times, even humorous. They also give some valuable information into what Bonhoeffer was reading while confined in his cell.

On Easter Sunday (25 April 1943), he assures his parents that even in Tegel he is having a happy Easter. He writes about how Good Friday and Easter 'free us to think about other things far beyond our personal fate, about the ultimate meaning of life, suffering and events; and we lay hold of a great hope'. He acknowledges that he is being treated well, can smoke again (!) and is reading a good deal – newspapers, novels and, above all, the Bible.

In a letter of 15 May 1943 he tells his parents that he is reading the Bible through from cover to cover, and has just got as far as Job, 'which I am particularly fond of'. He writes that he reads the psalms very day: 'I know them and love them more than any other book.'

Bonhoeffer admits (4 June 1943) that 'joy is a thing we want very badly in this solemn building, where one never hears a laugh – it seems to get even the warders down'. Within the prison all was silent. One could hear nothing but the tramp of the prisoners pacing up and down their cells (14 June 1943). At this stage, Bonhoeffer is ten weeks in prison and is 'most grateful for anything that one can smoke'.

Knowing Bonhoeffer's ultimate fate, as we do, it is especially moving to see him write to his parents (24 July 1943):

Each time I write, I hope it will be my last letter to you from prison. Of course, this really becomes more likely every day; and one gradually gets sick of being here.

Bonhoeffer's parents were allowed to visit him from time to time. One such visit prompts him to write (17 August 1943):

The hour with you yesterday was again indescribably beautiful; thank you very much for coming ... the threat of bombs makes every day long [the Allied bombing of Berlin had begun] ... The day when we shall meet again in freedom gets closer and closer, and it will be one of those days which we shall never forget all our lives.

Especially moving are Bonhoeffer's references to Maria in a letter to his parents (5 September 1943):

> It makes me very happy to imagine Maria sewing and working away at the trousseau – really making preparations for the day. I can't do anything here but wait, hope and look forward to it.

According to Maria herself (Appendix to *Letters and Papers from Prison*), Bonhoeffer was given permission to write a one-page letter every four days, alternating between his parents and herself. Finally, he found a friendly guard who smuggled letters in both directions. Most of Bonhoeffer's letters to Maria are now in the Houghton Library at Harvard University. Maria remembers from her visits to Tegel that Bonhoeffer's reaction to imprisonment took on two forms, either confident hope that the end was clearly in sight, or utter annoyance at the fact that not enough pressure was applied to drive his case ahead. During Maria's visits, Bonhoeffer talked about details of their wedding; he had chosen the 103rd Psalm as a text and claimed that he was working on the menu.

After Bonhoeffer was moved to the Gestapo prison at Prinz-Albrecht-Strasse in October 1944 it was then impossible for Maria to obtain visitation permits, and improbable that any of her letters reached him. His last letter to Maria is dated 19 December 1944. In that letter, Bonhoeffer wrote:

> What is happiness and unhappiness? It depends so little on the circumstances; it depends only on that which happens inside a person. I am grateful every day that I have you, and that makes me happy.

In the book *Letters and Papers from Prison*, the majority of the long letters are written by Bonhoeffer to his friend and fellow theologian, Eberhard Bethge. Here, Bonhoeffer reveals more of his inner self and the sheer struggle of being confined in Tegel. On 15 December 1943, he writes to Bethge:

> I should at last have to start telling you that, in spite of everything that I've written so far, things here are revolting, that my grim experiences often pursue me into the night and that I can shake them off only by reciting

one hymn after another, ... I often wonder who I really am – the man who goes on squirming under these ghastly experiences in wretchedness that cries to heaven, or the man who scourges himself and pretends to others (and even to himself) that he is placid, cheerful, composed, and in control of himself, and allows people to admire him (i.e. for playing the part – or is it not playing a part?) ... In short, I know less than ever about myself ...

Some of the prisoners sought Bonhoeffer out to comfort them simply by having a chat. The nights around the end of January 1944, especially 30 January, were particularly bad with the bombing. Those prisoners who had been bombed out came to Bonhoeffer the next morning for a bit of comfort. He admits to Bethge (1 February 1944):

I'm afraid I'm bad at comforting; I can listen alright, but I can hardly ever find anything to say ... exact opposite.

Prisoners kept telling Bonhoeffer (Letter to Bethge, 30 April 1944) that he radiated so much peace around him and that he was always cheerful.

Bonhoeffer admits to Bethge that what is bothering him incessantly is the question of what Christianity really is, or indeed 'who Christ really is for us today.' Bonhoeffer feels that society is 'moving towards a completely religionless time'.

Even those who honestly describe themselves as 'religious' do not in the least act up to it...How is it, for example, that this war in contrast to all previous ones, is not calling forth any 'religious' reaction? ... What do a church, a community, a sermon, a liturgy, a Christian life mean in a religionless world?'

In a very moving passage in a letter to Bethge (16 July 1944), Bonhoeffer writes:

God would have us know that we must live as men who manage our lives without him. The God who is with us is the God who forsakes us (Mark 15:34) ... Before God and with God we live without God. God lets himself be pushed out of the world on the cross. He is weak and powerless in the world, and that is precisely the way, the only way, in which he is with us and helps us, not by virtue of his omnipotence, but by virtue of his weakness and suffering ... The Bible directs man to God's powerlessness and suffering; only the suffering God can help.'

Such thoughts must have brought Bonhoeffer some spiritual consolation in Tegel.

Bonhoeffer writes:

> Jesus asked in Gethsemane, 'Could you not watch with me one hour?' That is the reversal of what religious man expects from God. Man is summoned to share in God's sufferings at the hands of a godless world ... It is not the religious act that creates the Christian, but participation in the sufferings of God in the secular life. That is *metanoia* ... allowing oneself to be caught up in the way of Jesus Christ ... The 'religious act' is always something partial; 'faith' is something whole, involving the whole of one's life. Jesus calls men, not to a new religion, but to life. (18 July 1944)

Bonhoeffer further develops this thought in a letter to Bethge (21 July 1944):

> I'm still discovering right up to this moment, that it is only by living completely in this world that one learns to have faith ... By this-worldliness I mean living unreservedly in life's duties, problems, successes and failures, experiences and perplexities. In so doing we throw ourselves completely into the arms of God ... watching with Christ in Gethsemane. That, I think, is faith, that is *metanoia (conversion)*; and that is how a man becomes a Christian.

In 'Outline for a Book', Bonhoeffer asks 'Who is God?' He is not talking about an abstract belief in God, in God's omnipotence etc. That is not a genuine experience of God, but a partial extension of the world. What is paramount is encounter with Jesus Christ – the experience that a transformation of all human life is given in that fact that 'Jesus is there for others'. His 'being there for others' is the experience of transcendence. It is only this 'being there for others', maintained till death, that is the ground of Jesus' omnipotence and omnipresence. Faith is participation in this being of Jesus (incarnation, cross, resurrection) ... Our relation to God is a new life in 'existence for others', through participation in the being of Jesus.

Reflecting on the Church, Bonhoeffer holds that the Church is only the Church when it exists for others. As a challenge, he suggests that it should give away all its property to those in need. The clergy must live solely on the free-will offerings of their congregations, or possibly engage in some secular calling. The Church, according to Bonhoeffer, must share in secular problems of ordinary life, not dominating, but helping and serving. The Church's mission is to tell people what it means to live in Christ, to exist for others.

Bonhoeffer admits to Bethge that all that he has written in these letters about God, Christ and Church is still 'very crude and condensed' but that they are certain things that he was anxious to say simply and clearly. He hopes that they will be of some help for the Church's future.

In one of the last letters to Bethge, we see again how Christocentric Bonhoeffer's thought is:

All that we may rightly expect from God and ask him for, is to be found in Jesus Christ ... We must persevere in quiet meditation on the life, sayings, deeds, sufferings and death of Jesus ... danger and distress can only drive us closer to him ... It is certain that our joy is hidden in suffering, and our life in death; it is certain that in all this we are in a fellowship that sustains us ... If Jesus Christ had not lived, then our life would be meaningless, in spite of all the other people whom we know and honour and love.

The last letter to Bethge (23 August 1944) is especially moving, given that we know Bonhoeffer's ultimate fate. He asks Bethge not to get anxious or worried about him, but not to forget to pray for him. Bonhoeffer continues:

I am so sure of God's guiding hand that I hope that I shall always be kept in the certainty. You must never doubt that I'm travelling with gratitude and cheerfulness along the road where I'm being led. My past is brim-full of God's goodness, and my sins are covered by the forgiving love of Christ crucified. I am most thankful for the people I have met, and I only hope that they never have to grieve about me, but that they, too, will always be certain of and thankful for God's mercy and forgiveness.

Dietrich Bonhoeffer was surely a man who adopted Christ, the man for others, as his model, and gave witness to the cost of Christian discipleship to the very end.

# Reflection

Each new day is a new beginning in our life. Each day is a self-contained whole. Today is the limit of our cares and concerns. Today is long enough to find God or to lose God, to keep the faith or to succumb to sin and shame.

Just as the sun is new each day it rises, so too the eternal mercy of God is new every morning. To understand God's old faithfulness anew every morning, to be able to begin a new life with God in the midst of a life with God, is the gift God gives us every morning.

When we wake we can drive away the dark shades of night and the confusions of our dreams by immediately uttering the morning blessing and commending ourselves on this day to the help of the triune God.

Before the ear perceives the countless voices of the day it must listen in the early morning to the voice of the Creator and Redeemer. God has prepared the stillness of the earliest morning for himself. It must belong to God.

# CHAPTER THREE

# Pope John XXIII
### (1881–1963)

## Childhood

Angelo Giuseppe Roncalli was born on 25 November 1881 in the village of Sotto il Monte, about ten miles from Bergamo and some thirty-five miles north-east of Milan. He was one of thirteen children. His father, Giovanni Battista, was a small farmer. The land worked by the Roncalli family was not very productive and it was difficult to make ends meet. They managed to maintain a vineyard and some cornfields and they kept cattle.

## Minor and major seminary

In 1892, eleven-year-old Angelo entered the minor seminary in Bergamo. In 1895, he progressed to the major seminary and he received the clerical habit. As an adolescent, he was called '*il pretino*' – 'the little priest' – by his family.

At the end of 1895, Angelo began to write *Journal of a Soul*, a journal that he kept his entire life. It took different forms – a spiritual journal; entries from retreats and spiritual exercises; resolutions and day-by-day appointments, meetings and remarkable events of the day. He kept this journal until 1962, a few months before his death at the age of eighty-one. It therefore embraces a span of sixty-seven years. Much of the information in this chapter is gleaned from this source.

The young Angelo was deeply influenced by his Uncle Zaverio, who participated in the beginning of the Catholic Action Movement in Bergamo – a movement that focused on justice for workers. Zaverio also introduced Angelo to the spirituality of the bishop of Geneva, St Francis de Sales (1567–1622) and St John Bosco (1815–1888).

Angelo's favourite Frenchman was St Francis de Sales, whose sensible, cheerful advice he read over and over. In his *Journal of a Soul*, Angelo referred to Francis as 'my St. Francis de Sales ... my special protector and particular model'. He wrote of Francis:

> What a magnificent figure of a man, priest, bishop! If I were like him, I would not mind even if they made me Pope! ... My life, so the Lord tells me, must be a perfect copy of that of St. Francis de Sales if I wish to bear good fruits ... Nothing extraordinary in me or in my behaviour, except my way of doing ordinary things ... all ordinary things but done in no ordinary way ... Unalterable serenity of mind, wonderful gentleness with all, that is all.

The above passage reveals Angelo's appropriation of key dimensions of the style of spirituality of Francis de Sales – gentleness, humility, peacefulness, doing small things with deep love – virtues that would later mark his style of loving service as pope.

In an entry for 1896, when he was fifteen, Angelo writes that he will make every effort to mortify himself, above all and at all times chastising his self-love, his 'besetting sin'. He felt that he needed to curb his 'desire to show off, to hold people's attention or to attach any importance to myself'. It is amusing to read an entry for 1898 where he writes: 'I thought I could have been a saint by this time, and instead I am as miserable as before.' He was only eighteen! His greatest fault, according to himself, was 'wanting to be Solomon, to sit in judgement, to lay down the law left and right'.

From 1901–04, Angelo was studying in Rome at the Seminario Romano. On 10 August 1904, he was ordained priest in the Church of Santa Maria in Monte Santo in Piazza del Popolo in Rome. On the afternoon of his ordination, he returned to his seminary room to write to his bishop and his parents. He later visited his favourite churches and the altars of his favourite saints – St Philip Neri, St Ignatius Loyola, St Aloysius Gonzaga, St John Berchmans, St Catherine of Siena, St Camillus de Lellis. The following day, he celebrated his first Mass at a side altar in St Peter's. Towards midday, he had an audience with Pope Pius X, who addressed kind words of encouragement to him. Around the time of his ordination we find a journal entry:

> What shall become of me in the future? Will I become a good theologian, a jurist, a country priest, a bishop, a cardinal, a pope, or a simple poor priest? ... My God is everything ... The good Jesus will send up in smoke my ideals of ambition and reputation before the world.

In July 1904, Angelo received his doctorate in theology. The examiner for his written exam was Eugenio Pacelli, the future Pope Pius XII.

## The young priest – Bergamo and Rome

In 1905, Angelo was appointed secretary to the new bishop of Bergamo, Bishop Giacomo Radini Tedeschi. This appointment was to prove a transformative experience for Angelo as a priest and as an intellectual. Bishop Tedeschi was engaged with the social aspect of Italian Catholicism, convinced of the need for a 'pastoral modernity' in the Church. He gave his moral and financial support to the workers on strike at the cotton factory in Rancia (a strike that lasted for fifty days in 1909). He sent some of his priests to study in Jerusalem and in Louvain, one of the most important centres of the liturgical movement at the beginning of the twentieth century.

A crucial experience for the young Fr Angelo Roncalli was pastoral visitation. From December 1905 through the end of 1906, Roncalli accompanied Bishop Tedeschi on visits to the 350 parishes of the diocese. In a diary entry for 8 December 1905, he asks:

> What is the 'pastoral visit'? It is the friend who goes to a friend, the doctor to the infirm, the captain to the soldiers, the shepherd to the flock, the father to the children. The bishop is all this and here is the concept of the pastoral visit.

We will see that Roncalli tried to be all of the above in the various assignments that would be given him, culminating in his election as pope in 1958.

Between 1906 and 1914, Roncalli taught Church history in the seminary at Bergamo. This was the time of the anti-Modernist movement in the Church. Modernism had been condemned by two Vatican documents released in 1907; one from the Holy Office and the other from Pope Pius X himself. Concerns over Modernism expressed the worry that modern historical, scientific and philosophical currents were infecting the Church's ability faithfully to transmit divine revelation and the truths of the faith. Roncalli himself was accused of transmitting 'modernist heresy' in his lectures! News of the accusation came while he was attending a number of meetings in Rome in June 1914. In a disturbing meeting with Cardinal De Lai, Secretary for Seminaries, the Cardinal recommended that 'the young professor at Bergamo exercise extreme caution in his teaching'. Roncalli was deeply wounded by these accusations and sought solace by praying at the tomb of St Ignatius Loyola in the Jesuit Church of the Gesù.

Italy did not enter the First World War until 1915 and, in May, Roncalli was called to serve as a military chaplain, which he did until 1918. He served part-time at the military hospital in Bergamo as a reserve sergeant. He was still able to continue his intellectual work; he taught in the seminary in Bergamo and, in 1916, published a biography of Bishop Radini Tedeschi, who had died in 1914.

On 3 November, 1919, Roncalli wrote in his journal:

> The more I go on in life, the less attracted I feel to the Roman milieu. I am comfortable there as a pilgrim, but now I would not want to live there permanently, even if I see the immense good that needs to be done.

## The call to Rome

Ironically, in 1920, Roncalli received a letter from Cardinal Van Rossam, Prefect of the Congregation for the Propagation of the Faith, appointing him Secretary for the Propagation of the Faith in Italy, which necessitated living in Rome. Roncalli arrived in the city on 18 January 1921 and stayed for four years. The period 1921–25 was crucial for Italian history; the Fascist Party took power and Italy was under the dictatorship of Benito Mussolini.

## Bulgaria

In February 1925, the Cardinal Secretary of State, Pietro Gasparri, summoned Roncalli to the Vatican and informed him of Pope Pius XI's decision to appoint him Apostolic Visitor to Bulgaria, which meant that he had to be ordained bishop. He was about to begin a very long period (almost thirty years) in which he would be far from Italy – and far from Rome, in particular. He spent the next twenty years in Eastern Europe, serving more than nine years in Bulgaria and then another nine in Turkey.

Bulgaria was very much a secondary destination on the peripheries of the Roman Catholic Church. Bulgarian Catholics numbered only about 35,000. In 1923, there had been a coup d'état which banned all democratic parties and, when Roncalli arrived in Sofia, the country was politically very tense. Ten days before his arrival there, the capital was the target of a terrorist attack that blew up the cathedral of Sofia and claimed 120 lives.

In those tense and unecumenical times, Roncalli was not always greeted warmly. He was the first papal representative resident in Bulgaria in more than five centuries. He was initially seen by some of the Orthodox Christians as part of an insidious plot to convert Orthodox believers to Roman Catholicism. Nevertheless, he developed positive personal relationships with many Orthodox Church leaders by the diplomacy of brotherly love. He embarked on pastoral visits by mule, cart and raft. He also developed a good relationship with the Orthodox Bulgarian king, Boris III.

Roncalli's major problem in Bulgaria was the silence from Rome, even when he asked for help or feedback on his initiatives. He wrote:

> My ministry has given me many tribulations. But ironically they do not come from the Bulgarians, but from the Roman Curia. It is a mortification and humiliation that I did not expect, and it hurts me very much.

In the summer of 1925, Roncalli showed his irritation when he wrote to the Roman Curial Congregation for Extraordinary Ecclesiastical Affairs:

> I know that in Rome it takes time to make decisions. But at least a few words to give me some idea about the general horizons of my mission … or at least invite me to be patient … or give me a tip on some event or personal matter for which I begged and pleaded … But nothing …

Roncalli's frustration also emerges from notes that he wrote in his journal during a retreat from 28 April to 4 May 1930:

> The trials, with which in recent months the Lord has tested my patience, have been many … the uncertainty which has now lasted for more than five years about the exact scope of my mission in this country; my frustrations and disappointments at not being able to do more, and my enforced restriction to my life of a complete hermit, in opposition to work directly ministering to souls.

One of the similes used by St Francis de Sales which Roncalli loved to repeat when he was suffering in Bulgaria was: 'I am like a bird singing in the thicket of thorns.' He felt that this saying must be a continual inspiration to him to say very little about the things that hurt him but that he must show great discretion and forbearance in his judgements of people and situations.

# Turkey and Greece

On 17 November 1934, Roncalli was appointed apostolic visitor to Turkey and Greece. His official residence would be in Istanbul. In Turkey, there were only about 30,000 Catholics of different rites – Armenian, Chaldean, Greek, Syriac and Melkite. They were mostly French-speaking, and non-Turkish by ethnic origin.

The regime of Mustafa Kemal Atatürk (father of the Turks), who took over Turkey after the collapse of the Ottoman Empire at the end of the First World War, was marked by a visible and ideological secularist agenda, effectively banning every religious presence from the public square in an attempt to modernise the country via an eradication of the public role of Islam. All clergy were ordered to wear civilian attire.

Roncalli studied Turkish in order to do both his work as a papal diplomat and a Catholic archbishop with pastoral duties. In October 1936, he wrote of being 'fond of the Turks'. He saw learning the Turkish language as his special intention and an exercise in mortification! In 1936, he also made a pilgrimage to Mount Athos and even managed to stay in Greece (a country that was particularly difficult for a Vatican diplomat to enter) for a few weeks.

Roncalli discouraged the conversions of Orthodox Christians to Roman Catholicism. He wanted prospective converts to go deeper in the understanding of their own Orthodox tradition, which he did not see as schismatic.

The death of Pope Pius XI and the subsequent election of Pius XII, on 2 March 1939, gave Roncalli the opportunity to send a message to the Orthodox Patriarchate of Constantinople. It was the first official exchange between the Roman Catholic Church and the Orthodox Church since they had excommunicated each other in 1054! In May 1939, Roncalli actually met with the Patriarch of Constantinople, an historical achievement.

During the Second World War, Turkey remained neutral. Roncalli's network of contacts proved crucial to his effort to save Jewish refugees from Eastern Europe. He participated in several secret missions to save approximately 24,000 Jews.

# Nuncio to Paris

On 6 December 1944, while in Istanbul, Roncalli received a telegram from Rome announcing his appointment as apostolic nuncio to Paris. When he arrived at the airport in Paris on 30 December, nobody was there to meet him. It was a sign of the isolation that would be part of his eight years in Paris.

His first and most urgent issue was the request of General de Gaulle for the resignation of twenty-four bishops that the 'new France' determined had been too involved with the Vichy government during German occupation of France in the Second World War. Roncalli managed through diplomatic means to have only four bishops leave their dioceses. He convinced the four bishops to retire voluntarily and the Vatican appointed four bishops to replace them.

From 1945 onwards, Roncalli often mentions the approach of old age. In 1945 itself there is an entry which goes: 'I am definitely approaching old age. My mind resents this and almost rebels, for I still feel young, agile and alert. But one look in the mirror disillusions me.' In 1947, he writes: 'Now I am in my sixty-seventh year, anything may happen.' In 1950, we have the entry:

> When one is nearly seventy, one cannot be too sure of the future. My spiritual life must be intensified. No overloading with devotions of a novel and secondary character, but fidelity to those that are fundamental – Holy Mass, the Breviary, the Rosary, meditations, the reading of good books, close and frequent union with Jesus in the Blessed Sacrament.

There is a rather moving story of Roncalli's conversation with a professor at a reception in Paris. The professor requested that they speak only about French literature since he did not believe in God anymore. Roncalli agreed, but in the course of the conversation, the professor mentioned that his mother prayed the Rosary regularly. Roncalli said, 'Oh please give my blessings to your mother.' The professor asked: 'Excellency, do you really believe in God?' Roncalli replied: 'I do not believe in God. I see God. I see God in your mother who says the Rosary. I see God in a little sick baby. Professor, with the prayers of your mother, one day you also will see God.' After Pope John's death, his secretary, Monsignor Capovilla, met the professor quite by chance and the professor said to Capovilla: 'Today I see God.'

## Patriarch of Venice

On 12 January 1953, Roncalli, aged seventy-one, was appointed Patriarch of Venice. He arrived in Venice on 15 March. Commenting on his appointment as Cardinal and Patriarch of Venice, Roncalli notes in his journal that he is thrilled to be back in pastoral work. In his first address in St Mark's Basilica in Venice, he spoke to the people as a friend and shepherd:

> I want to talk to you with great frankness. You have waited for me impatiently. Things have been said and written about me that greatly exaggerate my merits. I humbly introduce myself ... I humbly commend to your benevolence the man who simply wants to be your brother, amiable, approachable and understanding ... Therefore, do not look at your patriarch as a politician, as a diplomat; look for the priest, the shepherd of souls, who exercises his office among you in the name of the Lord.

Roncalli soon realised that he had two painful problems amid all the splendour of ecclesiastical state, and the veneration shown to him as Cardinal and Patriarch – the scantiness of his revenue and the throng of poor folk with their requests for employment and financial help.

Again, Roncalli, during his annual retreat from 20–25 May 1955, writes in *Journal of a Soul* of his advancing years and the thought of death which 'has kept me good'. In the space of seventeen months, three of his dear sisters had died, 'two of them especially dear because they lived solely for the Lord and for me; for more than thirty years they looked after my house (Ancilla and Maria looked after his house in Sotto il Monte). Losing them has been a great blow to me ... '.

As events would turn out, it is somewhat ironic that we find Roncalli writing in September 1958 that his advanced age should make him more cautious in accepting preaching engagements outside his diocese. He finds that he has to write everything down first, and this is a great effort, 'besides the constant humiliation of feeling my own insufficiency. May the Lord help me and forgive me.'

Pope Pius XII died on 9 October 1958. Before boarding the train in Venice that would carry him to Rome and to the papal conclave, Roncalli said: 'We are not here to guard a museum, but to cultivate a flourishing garden of life.' One can almost hear echoes of some of the statements of Pope Francis. Incidentally, Roncalli had bought his return ticket to Venice!

## Pope

The conclave was small – fifty-one cardinals, eighteen of them Italian. On 28 October 1958, Roncalli was elected on the eleventh vote. He was seventy-seven years of age. The cardinals thought that he would be a 'pope of transition'. As one French abbot commented:

> What we need is an old man, a transitional pope. He won't introduce any great innovations, and will give us time to pause and reorganise. In that way, the real choices that cannot be made now will be postponed.

The Holy Spirit had other plans!

Cardinal Roncalli chose the name John, although he knew that there had been an anti-pope, John XXIII (1410–15) in Avignon. John was also the name of his father, of the patron saint of his birthplace, of the Baptist and of the evangelist.

In his papacy, Pope John XXIII wanted to prioritise the simple but profound exhortation of 1 John 4:7–8: 'Beloved, let us love one another, because love is from God. Whoever does not love does not love God, for God is love.' During his coronation, Pope John emphasised his commitment to being a good pastor in the manner of the description of the Good Shepherd in John's Gospel, stressing that the other human qualities – knowledge, shrewdness, diplomatic tact, organisational abilities – can help the pope carry out his office, but they can be no substitute for his task as a pastor.

John XXIII's coronation took place in the central loggia of the Vatican on 4 November 1958, the feast of St Charles Borromeo. He was crowned with the 1877 Palatine Tiara and his coronation ran for the traditional five hours.

Near the beginning of his tenure, Pope John confessed to his private secretary, Monsignor Capovilla, that he was lonely and could not get used to eating alone, a practice maintained by his predecessor, Pius XII. He began to invite cardinals and visiting bishops to dine with him. When someone reminded him of the solitary habits of Pope Pius XII, John responded: 'I value tradition and I grant that my predecessors did too. I must confess, however, that I have never found any place in the Bible which suggests that the Pope should eat alone.'

On Christmas Day 1958, Pope John became the first pope since 1870 to make pastoral visits in his diocese of Rome, when he visited children with polio at the Bambino Gesù Hospital. The following day, he visited Rome's Regina Coeli prison, where he told the inmates: 'You could not come to me, so I came to you.' Such gestures created a sensation in the media.

Although official diplomatic ties were not established between the Vatican and Israel until 1993, Pope John paved the way for healing historical wounds and establishing friendlier relations with the Jewish people. During the Second World War, John participated in several secret missions to save approximately 24,000 Jews. He greeted a visiting delegation of Jewish rabbis as newly elected pope with the words: 'I am Joseph, your brother' – 'Joseph' was his second name. During his first Easter season as pope, John ordered that the phrase 'perfidious Jews' be removed from the Good Friday liturgy.

In *Journal of a Soul*, John tells us that 'without any forethought, I put forward, in one of my first talks with my Secretary of State, on 20 January 1959, the idea of an Ecumenical Council ... '. John adds: 'I was the first to be surprised at my proposal which was entirely my own.' The decision to call the Council was announced on 25 January 1959 at the end of the Week of Prayer for Christian Unity and in the Basilica of St Paul-outside-the-Walls. Some of the cardinals present received the news with a deafening silence.

In his first encyclical, *Ad Petri Cathedram* (29 June 1959), Pope John wrote:

> The Catholic Church, of course, leaves many questions open to the discussion of theologians ... far from jeopardizing the Church's unity, controversies, as noted English author, Cardinal Newman, has remarked, can actually pave the way for its attainment. For discussion can lead to fuller and deeper understanding of religious truths; when one strikes against another, there may be a spark'. (71)

Pope John recommends the primacy of charity in scholarly and ecclesial endeavours. He reminds his readers of the saying of the medieval St Bernard of Clairvaux: 'in essentials unity; in doubtful matters liberty; in all things charity'.

On 2 December 1960, Pope John met the Anglican Primate, Archbishop Geoffrey Fisher, at the Vatican. Such a meeting between a pope and an archbishop of Canterbury had not taken place for 400 years.

Pope John decided to expand the College of Cardinals beyond the limit of seventy established by Pope Sixtus V in 1586, increasing it to eighty-five. He used the opportunity to name the first cardinals from Africa, Japan and the Philippines. He created fifty-two cardinals in five consistories that included his successor Pope Paul VI.

During the days of the Cuban Missile Crisis (16–29 October 1962), Pope John was personally involved in offering the US and the Soviet Union a channel of communication in order to avoid a nuclear holocaust. He wrote his appeal for negotiations. He sent a message to US President John F. Kennedy and the Soviet leader, Nikita Khrushchev, reminding them of their grave responsibilities and begging them for peace. Within hours of airing the message on Vatican Radio, Soviet ships returned home. Pope John became *Time* magazine's 'Man of the Year'. He was the first pope to receive the title, and was followed by John Paul II in 1994 and Francis in 2013.

The Vatican Council began on 11 October 1962. In his opening address, Pope John said that the Church must communicate a predominantly pastoral view of the Church's teaching office, preferring the 'medicine of mercy' over 'weapons of severity', persuasion over condemnation. The pastoral vocabulary of the Council would emphasise invitation, persuasion, dialogue, active engagement and the willingness to learn. There would be no condemnation of other faiths and practices in the documents of the Council.

On 5 March 1963, John received in audience Nikita Khrushchev's daughter and her husband. They were the first Soviet citizens admitted into the Vatican since the Russian Revolution in 1917.

On 11 April 1963, live on Italian television, Pope John signed his encyclical *Pacem in Terris* (*Peace on Earth*). In a press conference the week before, he said: 'Some say the Pope is too optimistic ... but I cannot be different from our Lord, who spreads goodness, joy, peace and encouragement.'

The last time Pope John spoke to the faithful gathered in St Peter's Square was on 22 May 1963, the evening of the Feast of the Ascension. He greeted the crowds with a wide gesture and recited the Marian prayer: 'O Queen of Heaven, rejoice, alleluia.' He ended with the greeting: 'Saluti, saluti.'

When John XXIII received the Sacrament of the Sick on his deathbed, all around were weeping. Thereupon he, knocking repeatedly on the wooden part of his bed, exclaimed, 'Coraggio, It's not yet the Requiem!' The Jews of the community of Rome came to St Peter's Square to pray the Psalms for the dying Pope.

Pope John XXIII died on 3 June 1963 at 7.45 pm. His last words were: 'Mater mea, fiducia mea' ('My mother, my trust'). His cause for canonisation was opened on 18 November 1965 by his successor, Pope Paul VI, during the final session of the Second Vatican Council. Pope Paul declared him a Servant of God. Pope John was beatified by Pope John Paul II on 3 September 2000 and was canonised, along with Pope John Paul II, by Pope

Francis on 27 April 2014. The date assigned for the liturgical celebration of John XXIII is not 3 June, the anniversary of his death, as would be usual, but 11 October, the anniversary of his opening of the Second Vatican Council.

## Epilogue

I cannot conclude this very brief portrait of Pope John XXIII without making reference to his well-known sense of humour – an essential quality in the spiritual life. Two anecdotes must suffice. On the morning after his election, the story goes, Pope John appeared briefly in public at a side-entrance to St Peter's, leading on to a street. He mingled with the crowd. On seeing him, one lady was heard to say to her friend: 'My God, he's so fat!' Pope John, overhearing the comment, turned to the lady and said: 'Signora, the papal conclave isn't exactly a beauty contest.'

Pope John liked to make surprise visits to certain places in Rome, especially to hospitals and prisons. He once paid a surprise visit to the Hospital of the Holy Spirit. A young nun, seeing the papal entourage draw up at the hospital entrance, ran up to the office of the Superior to break the news. The Superior rose from her desk, ran down the stairs to the hospital entrance, flung herself at the feet of Pope John to kiss the papal ring and said: 'Your Holiness, I am the Superior of the Holy Spirit', to which the Pope is reputed to have replied: 'I must say you are most fortunate. I only happen to be the Vicar of Jesus Christ!'

Having reflected on his life in these few pages, it is no wonder that John XXIII is affectionately known as the 'Good Pope' and, in Italian, 'Il Papà Buono'.

## Reflection

May everyone be able to say of me that I have never sowed dissension and mistrust. That I have never grieved anyone by engendering suspicion or fear; that I have been frank, loyal, trusting; that I have looked into the eyes of others with sympathy, even those persons who do not share my ideals, so as not to hinder the realisation of the greatest commandment of Jesus: That they all be one!

CHAPTER FOUR

# Thomas Merton
(1915–1968)

## Childhood

Thomas Merton was born in Prades, Pyrénées-Orientales, southern France, on 31 January 1915, to Owen Merton, a New Zealand painter active in Europe and the US, and Ruth Jenkins, an American Quaker and artist. Thomas was baptised in the Church of England, in accordance with his father's wishes. Ruth did not want any spurious religious influences brought to bear until Thomas was of an age to decide for himself.

During the First World War, in August 1915, the Merton family left France for the US. They lived first with Ruth's parents in Queens, New York, and then settled near them in Douglaston. In 1917, the family moved to Flushing, Queens, where Thomas's brother John Paul was born on 2 November 1918. The family was considering returning to France when Ruth was diagnosed with stomach cancer. Ruth wrote Thomas a letter from Bellevue Hospital. 'My mother was informing me by mail that she was about to die and would never see me again.' She died on 21 October 1921. Thomas was six years old and his brother not yet three.

In 1922, Owen took Thomas with him on a trip to Bermuda where Owen fell in love with the American novelist Evelyn Scott. Still grieving for his mother, Thomas never quite warmed to Scott. Happy to get away from her, Thomas was returned to Douglaston in 1923 at the age of eight to live with his mother's family, who were also caring for his brother.

In 1925, having travelled through France, Italy, England and Algeria, Owen returned to New York to pick up Thomas, bringing his son to live in Saint-Antonin, southern France. Thomas returned to France with mixed feelings, as he had lived with his grandparents for the last two years and had become attached to them.

In 1926, when Thomas was eleven, Owen enrolled him in a boy's boarding school in Mountauban, the Lycée Ingres. There, Thomas felt lonely, depressed and abandoned. During his initial months at the school, he begged his father to remove him. With time, however, he grew comfortable with his surroundings. He befriended a circle of aspiring writers at the Lycée and wrote two novels!

Meanwhile, Owen was travelling, painting and attending to an exhibition of his work in London. In the summer of 1928, he withdrew Thomas from the Lycée Ingres, saying they were moving to England. They lived with Owen's aunt and uncle in Ealing, West London. Thomas was soon enrolled in Ripley Court Preparatory School, a boarding school in Surrey. Toward the end of 1929, Owen took Thomas with him to live in Scotland. Owen became ill and was diagnosed with a brain tumour.

In 1930, Thomas was boarded at Oakham School in Rutland, England. Owen died on 16 January 1931. Thomas was assured by his grandfather Merton that he would provide for the youth and Tom Bennett, Owen's physician, became Thomas's legal guardian. Bennett allowed Merton to use his unoccupied house in London during the holidays.

## Travels and Cambridge

In September 1932, Thomas passed the entrance examination for Clare College, Cambridge. He toured Europe: travelling to Paris and Marseille and going by train to Genoa, Florence and Rome. In February 1933, Merton lived in a small pensione by the Palazzo Barberini in Rome. He came to appreciate the beauty of the city. He was drawn to its varied, ancient churches. He read the New Testament from the Latin Vulgate. He confronted the emptiness of his life, and began to pray more regularly. He visited Tre Fontane, a Trappist monastery in Rome, where he first thought of becoming a Trappist monk.

Merton sailed by ship from Italy to the US to visit his Jenkins grandparents in Douglaston for the summer, before entering Clare College. He continued to read his Latin bible. At the end of the summer he returned to England.

In October 1933, Merton, now eighteen, entered Clare College as an undergraduate to study French and Italian. In his later autobiography, *The Seven Storey Mountain*, Merton wrote that his time at Cambridge became the 'pit of hell'. He did not achieve good grades in his examinations and was in danger of losing his scholarship. He lost any sense of direction in his life. Some acquaintances saw him as a womaniser. He spent so freely that his guardian Bennett summoned him to London to try to talk sense to him. Most of Merton's biographers agree that Merton fathered a child with a woman with whom he had a liaison at Cambridge. Bennett discreetly settled a threatened legal action. This child has never been identified in published accounts. Some accounts suggest that the young woman and baby were later killed in the Blitz in London, but there is no definitive proof of this.

Merton's guardian, Bennett, had had enough. In a meeting in April, he arranged with Merton for his return to the US, promising not to tell his Jenkins grandparents about his excesses. In May 1934, Merton left Cambridge after completing his exams.

## Columbia University

In January 1935, Merton, aged twenty-one, enrolled as a sophomore at Columbia University in Manhattan. He lived with his Jenkins grandparents in Douglaston, travelling daily by train and subway to the Columbia campus. In October 1935, he joined the local peace movement, having taken 'the Oxford Pledge' against supporting any government in any war.

In 1936, Merton's grandfather, Samuel Jenkins, died. In February 1937, Merton read *The Spirit of Medieval Philosophy* by Étienne Gilson, which enlarged his sense of Catholicism. Gilson wrote that the notion of God articulated by Thomas Aquinas and others was that God was the source of all being and that all other beings participated in God's being. Merton wrote: 'For the first time in my life I began to realize that everything was interconnected.' In August 1937, Merton's grandmother, known to the family as Bonne Maman, died.

In January 1938, Merton graduated from Columbia with a BA in English. He continued there, starting graduate work in English. He began to read *The Confessions of Saint Augustine* and *The Imitation of Christ*. He decided to explore Catholicism further. Finally, in August 1938, he decided to attend Mass and went to Corpus Christi Church, located near the Columbia campus.

## Becoming a Roman Catholic

One evening in September 1938, Merton was reading about Gerard Manley Hopkins's conversion to Catholicism and becoming a priest. Suddenly,

Merton could not shake the sense that he, too, should follow such a path. He realised that Hopkins had made a spontaneous decision to become a Roman Catholic and, as Merton writes in *The Seven Storey* Mountain, 'Why shouldn't I do the same?' He headed quickly to the Corpus Christi Church rectory, where he met Fr George Barry Ford, and expressed his desire to become a Catholic. In the following weeks Merton started catechism, learning the basics of his new faith. On 6 November 1938, he was baptised at Corpus Christi Church and received Holy Communion. It would seem that Catholicism attracted Merton first of all intellectually and then he became interested in its aesthetics– the beauty of its theology and spirituality and of its liturgy when well performed.

On 22 February 1939, Merton received his MA in English from Columbia University with a thesis on Nature and Art in the poetry of William Blake. He decided he would pursue his PhD at Columbia and moved from Douglaston to Greenwich Village. On 25 May 1939, Merton received Confirmation as a Catholic at Corpus Christi Church, and took the Confirmation name James.

## A possible priestly vocation?

Merton appreciated what he read about St Francis of Assisi and felt that he might have a vocation to the Franciscan way of life. Initially accepted to join the Franciscan novitiate in August 1940, Merton began to have some doubts. He felt that he had not been sufficiently honest and forthright in his interview. When he told Fr Edmund Murphy more about his past, Merton was told that he was not deemed suitable material for a vocation as a Franciscan friar. Merton now believed that his religious calling was finished.

In early August 1940, Merton got a job in the English Department of St Bonaventure University, a Franciscan establishment. While teaching at St Bonaventure's, Merton entered more deeply into his prayer life. He all but gave up drinking, quit smoking, stopped going to movies and became more selective in his reading. In April 1941, he went to a Holy Week retreat at the Abbey of Our Lady of Gethsemani near Bardstown, Kentucky.

On his return to St Bonaventure, with Gethsemani still on his mind, one evening he opened his Vulgate bible at random and his finger pointed to a line which read *'ecce eris tacens'* ('behold, you will be silent') – the words of the angel to Zechariah in the opening chapter of Luke's Gospel. Immediately, he thought of the Trappists at Gethsemani.

49

# The Abbey of Gethsemani

On 10 December 1941, Merton arrived at the Abbey of Gethsemani and spent three days at the monastery guest house, waiting for acceptance into the order. The novice master visited Merton to gauge his sincerity and qualifications, and on 13 December, he was accepted into the monastery as a postulant by Frederic Dunne, Gethsemani's abbot since 1935. Merton tells us that from the moment he entered the monastery he was overwhelmed with the holiness and sanctified atmosphere that filled it. He noted in his journal:

> This is the only real city in America. Now I know that the prayers of these monks are what is holding the world together.

He wrote that at Gethsemani he could finally 'stop arguing with the seven guys who argue inside my head and be completely quiet in front of the Face of Peace … These are the four walls of my new freedom.'

In March 1942, on the first Sunday of Lent, Merton was accepted as a novice at the monastery. In June, he received a letter from his brother John Paul stating that he was soon to leave for the war and would be coming to Gethsemani to visit before leaving. John Paul arrived on 17 June. He expressed his desire to become a Roman Catholic, and on 26 July was baptised at a church in nearby New Haven, Kentucky, leaving the following day. This would be the last time the two saw each other. John Paul died on 19 April 1943, when his plane failed over the English Channel.

## Merton – the writer

Merton's abbot, Dom Frederic Dunne, saw that Merton had both a gifted intellect and a talent for writing, and in 1943, he was tasked with translating religious texts and writing biographies of the saints for the monastery. On 19 March, he made his temporary profession. In November 1944, a book of poetry entitled *Thirty Poems* was published. Merton initially had mixed feelings about publishing his work, but Abbot Dunne remained resolute about Merton continuing his writing. In 1946, another book of poetry, *A Man in the Divided Sea* was published. The same year, Merton's manuscript for *The Seven Storey Mountain* was accepted for publication.

Merton's autobiography was written during two-hour intervals in the monastery scriptorium as a personal project.

By 1947 Merton was more comfortable in his role as a writer. On 19 March, he took his solemn vows, a commitment to live out his life at the monastery. He also began corresponding with a Carthusian at St Hugh's Charterhouse in England. Merton had harboured an appreciation for the Carthusians since coming to Gethsemani in 1941, and would later consider leaving the Trappists for that order.

In 1948 *The Seven Storey Mountain* was published to critical acclaim, with fan mail to Merton reaching new heights. Merton remarked: 'I am getting so much fan mail that it makes me nervous.' The autobiography was immediately praised by such eminent writers and novelists as Graham Greene and Evelyn Waugh. It sold over a hundred thousand copies in the first year alone.

Merton's abbot, Frederic Dunne, died on 3 August 1948, while travelling on a train to Georgia. Dunne's death was painful for Merton, who had come to look on the abbot as a father figure and spiritual mentor. On 15 August, the monastic community elected Dom James Fox, a former US Navy officer, as their new abbot. In October, Merton discussed with him his ongoing attraction to the Carthusian and Camaldolese orders and their eremitical way of life, to which Fox responded by assuring Merton that he belonged at Gethsemani. Fox permitted Merton to continue his writing.

In 1949, *Seeds of Contemplation, The Waters of Siloe* and the British edition of *The Seven Storey Mountain* (under the title *Elected Silence*) were published. On 26 May (Ascension Thursday) 1949, Merton was ordained priest, saying his first Mass the following day. Merton wrote of himself shortly after his ordination:

> There is practically nothing of the priest about me. I am still a rough diamond, without any gentleness or tact or charity. Well, the first apostles are my consolation. But I pray that I may imitate them as they were <u>after</u> Pentecost, not before!'

## Vocation to write

The poet Gerard Manley Hopkins gave up writing poetry when he became a Jesuit, feeling that the vocations of the priest and the poet were incompatible. Thankfully, Hopkins's superior later ordered him to begin to write again. Merton, at least early on, experienced something of the same tension between being a monk/priest and a writer. We read in a letter written in 1955:

> I have stopped writing, and that is a big relief. I intend to renounce it for good, if I can live in solitude. I realize that I have suffered more than I know from this 'writing career'. Writing is deep in my nature, and I cannot deceive myself that it will be easy for me to do without it. At least I can get along without the public and without my reputation! The whole business tends to corrupt the purity of one's spirit of faith. It obscured the view of God and of divine things.

The irony here is that it was through his books that Merton introduced vast numbers to the contemplative tradition within Christianity, especially to the writings of the Church Fathers and the great Christian mystics. Merton himself was often uncomfortable and dissatisfied with what he had written. In 1956, he wrote:

> I am awfully aware of the shallowness and superficiality of most of the writing I did between 1945 and 1950 … and some of what I have written since then too.

Even of *The Seven Storey Mountain* Merton said:

> … it is a sort of phenomenon, not all bad, not all good … Naturally I have reservations about it because I was young and I've changed …

Merton readily admitted: 'My writing has been a safety valve for my neurosis' (1956).

Despite all the inner conflict about which vocation to pursue – writer or monk/priest – it would seem that Merton came to some resolution of this issue in the early 1960s. In 1964, he is able to acknowledge:

> As I reflect over the past and over God's grace in my life there are two things that are more or less certain to me: that I have been called to be at once a writer and solitary *secundum quid* (in some way).

## Contemplative life and prayer

In November 1949, Merton started teaching spirituality to the novices at Gethsemani, a work he greatly enjoyed. Merton would later become

Master of Novices for ten years (1955–65). Paul Quenon, one of Merton's novices, said of him:

> The most important thing he taught me was how to love God and how to be true and honest in the presence of God. Not to fake it, just to be yourself and live in such a way that you know God accepts you and you go from there. Mostly he taught by example. There was no method. He never taught a method of prayer … He never gave any instructions except, 'Quieten down. Spend time in front of the Blessed Sacrament' or 'Go to the woods and just be quiet. Take a book and reflect on it'. Things like that. Real simple. It'll happen. That's the way he did it.

In 1964, Merton wrote of his approach to prayer for the novices:

> In the novitiate I don't use special methods. I try to make the novices love the freedom and peace of being with God alone in faith and simplicity, to abolish all divisiveness and diminish all useless strain and concentration on one's own efforts and all formalism …

At the core of Merton's spirituality lies the distinction between our real selves and our false selves. According to Merton,

> The false self … is the identity we assume in order to function in society, the springboard of all our egocentric desires for such things as honour, power and knowledge. We expend our energies constructing this nothingness into something objectively real. If we take the masks we daily wear to be our true faces, we will protect them with bandages of pleasures and glory, even at the cost of violating our own truth … But the real self towards which we should move, is a religious mystery, known in its entirety to God … The way to find the real 'world' is not by observing what is outside of us but about discovering *our own inner ground*. That is where the world is first and foremost – in our deepest selves to which we have our own unique doors.

For Merton the contemplative life meant a search for the essential truth of self and for God. He writes: 'The contemplative life means finding the true significance of my life, and my right place in God's creation. It means renouncing the way of life that is lived in the 'world' and which, to me, is a source of illusion, confusion and deception.' One of Merton's deceptively simple definitions of contemplation is:

> Just stop lying to yourself for twenty minutes. Just stop! Stop thinking and lying to yourself for twenty minutes and see what happens ... OK, what's reality? That's all I want. I don't want happiness, success, and these illusory things I think I need.

Merton is one of the exponents of the apophatic tradition in Christian spirituality, that is, a way of relating to God according to the belief that God cannot be conceptualised in human categories. Echoing the spirituality of St John of the Cross, Merton speaks of 'the curtain of darkness', 'the night of aridity' and 'the power of an obscure love'. In 1962, he wrote: 'There is an absolute need for the solitary, bare, dark, beyond-concept, beyond-thought, beyond feeling type of prayer.' Merton admits, 'Not, of course, for everyone ... About this I have no hesitations and no doubts, because it is my vocation.'

In 1967, Merton wrote:

> The contemplative is the person who has risked his/her mind in the desert beyond language and beyond ideas where God is encountered in the nakedness of pure trust ... The contemplative has nothing to tell you except to reassure you and say that if you dare to penetrate your own silence and risk the sharing of that solitude with the lonely other who seeks God through you, then you will truly recover the light and the capacity to understand what is beyond words and beyond explanations because it is too close to be explained: it is the intimate union in the depths of your own heart, of God's spirit and your own secret inmost self, so that you and God are all in truth One Spirit.

## Self-knowledge

It is striking how much importance the Christian mystics attach to self-knowledge. St Augustine went so far as to say that self-knowledge is God-knowledge. Growth in self-knowledge does not come without much interior struggle and often resistance. This is why God's grace is so essential here. Growing in self-knowledge was also a struggle for Merton. He wrote in a letter of 1956:

I am very happy that in all this wrestling with myself, I am really getting rid of an awful lot of Merton, but the void that replaces him is a bit disconcerting: except that I know that God is there. One thing is sure: I do not particularly want the survival of the person and even the writer I have been.

Merton admits that he projected his troubles onto everybody else – his mother, America, the monastery, the Church. He was conscious of being in 'hidden rebellion' against them all. He saw himself as 'boiling with hostilities and resistances which are an expression of my pride'. Merton writes in a letter of 1960 that he did not find it at all hard to hate himself. He particularly chastised himself about his lack of charity to the other monks: 'I like to flay them with words, and probably should feel more guilty about it than I do because here I sin and keep on sinning.'

Merton realised more and more that his big task was within himself. In 1960 he wrote:

I am seeing what are the depths of my pride, and what an obstacle it is … this tenacious attachment to self, and the virulence of it, which would make one stop at nothing in order to protect this inner root of self … Pray for me to be humble and really humble … with humility that is deep and afraid of nothing, of no truth, and which is completely abandoned to God's will. How hard that actually is.

Writing to an Islamic scholar, Abdul Aziz, in 1962, Merton said that the question of detachment depended on self-knowledge – or, rather, the two are mutually interdependent. In the same letter, he wrote that exterior detachment is easier: it is a matter of renouncing comforts and gratifications of the sensual appetite. But inner detachment 'centres around the 'self', especially one's pride, one's desire to react and to defend and to assert 'self' in one's own will. Merton asserted that this attachment to the 'self' is a fertile sowing ground for 'seeds of blindness'.

## Merton and nature

Merton's father taught him to look at the natural world and to celebrate his seeing. For Merton, this deep beholding of nature became an early way of praying. At Columbia University, Merton was an enthusiastic reader of

William Blake and other writers who viewed the natural world as numinous and epiphanies of the sacred. One of Blake's lines is 'All that is, is holy.' Merton used that line in a chapter heading in *Seeds of Contemplation*. He also borrowed the notion of 'inscape' from Gerard Manley Hopkins – that each created thing has its particular form that can be apprehended as vibrant and dynamic and emitting a numinous spirit life, almost as if everything had its own subjectivity.

In the 1950s Merton had the job of the abbey's forester, which afforded him new opportunities for solitude outside the monastic enclosure. He spoke of the forest as being 'his bride'. He is most light-hearted, most buoyant and jubilant, when he's writing about nature. He believed that it was the vocation of human persons to be 'gardeners of paradise'. We are to be 'celebrants of the natural world'. For Merton, paradise was this world fully beheld, fully beloved.

Merton is very much influenced here by the tradition of St Bonaventure (1221–1274), following St Augustine (354–430), about the 'vestiges of God' in creation, the vestiges of the Creator, the footprints of God in the natural world. St Francis de Sales has the same idea. Merton wrote in *Conjectures of a Guilty Bystander*: 'Paradise is all around us and we do not understand; we do not attend.'

Merton loved cats! He thought that people like dogs because they jump all over you and give you a lot of attention, whereas a cat is much more self-possessed. He said that the cat was a much more spiritual animal!

## Solitude

As we have already seen, Merton thought of becoming a Carthusian or a Camaldolese monk – their semi-eremitical lifestyle would have assured him of more solitude. One of Merton's many paradoxes was that, while he desired solitude, he also valued the company of friends whose conversations stimulated him. In 1963 he admitted that he was not the ideal of an absolute hermit:

> ... since my solitude is partly that of an intellectual and poet ... when I have continuous solitude for a more or less extended period, it means a great deal and is certainly the best remedy for the tensions and pressures that I generate when I am with the community.

He sensibly asserts that if you go into the desert merely to get away from people you dislike, 'you will find neither peace nor solitude, you will only isolate yourself with a tribe of devils'.

Merton finally achieved the solitude he had long desired while living in a hermitage on the monastery grounds in 1965. The hermitage was originally constructed by Merton and his novices on the pretext of having somewhere to meet ecumenical guests. It was also understood that Merton could use it for private purposes on occasion as well.

On 20 August 1965, Merton began living in the hermitage full time. That year he wrote that he liked being a hermit and having real solitude but the following year said, 'It is hard. You really have to face yourself and, believe me, that is quite grim'.

John Eudes Bamberger, one of Merton's former novices, said that Merton's need for solitude was not so much an evasion as it was a communion, a communing with life at a level where it spoke to him personally. Bamberger adds that Merton also needed people and that was his struggle, and that after Merton was in solitude for a certain time at Gethsemani, he began having too many visitors! Among Merton's visitors were Daniel Berrigan, the Jesuit priest and anti-Vietnam activist and the singer Joan Baez. He writes of Berrigan's visit: 'It was most stimulating. He is a man full of fire, the right kind, a real Jesuit, of which there are not too many perhaps!'

In subsequent years Merton would author many other books, amassing a wide readership. A person's place in society, views on social activism, and various approaches towards contemplative prayer and living became constant themes in his writings. During long years at Gethsemani, Merton changed from the passionately inward-looking young monk of *The Seven Storey Mountain* to a more contemplative writer and poet. He became well known for his dialogues with other faiths and his non-violent stand during the race riots and Vietnam War of the 1960s. By the 1960s, he was deeply concerned about the world and issues like peace, racial tolerance and social equality.

In April 1966, Merton underwent surgery to treat debilitating back pain. While recuperating in a Louisville hospital, he fell in love with Margie Smith, a student nurse assigned to his care. He referred to her in his diary as 'M'. He wrote poems to her and reflected on the relationship in 'A Midsummer Diary for M', The relationship petered out with Merton's return to the monastery

# Journey to Asia and sudden death

At the end of 1968, the new abbot, Flavian Burns, allowed Merton the freedom to undertake a tour of Asia, during which he met the Dalai Lama in India on three occasions, followed by a solitary retreat near Darjeeling, India.

On 10 December 1968, Merton was at a retreat centre named Sawang Kaniwat in Samut Prakan, a province near Bangkok, Thailand, attending a monastic conference. After giving a talk in the morning session, he was found dead later in the afternoon in the room of his cottage, lying on his back with a short-circuited floor fan lying across his body. His associate, the spiritual writer Jean Leclercq, states: 'In all probability the death of Thomas Merton was due in part to heart failure, in part to an electric shock.' There was a Benedictine nun present at the conference who, before she became a religious, was an Austrian physician and specialist in internal medicine. She determined that Merton had died from the effects of electric shock.

Merton's body was flown back to the US on board a military aircraft returning from Vietnam. He is buried at Gethsemani Abbey.

# Letters and journals

The letters of Thomas Merton, which are archived at the Thomas Merton Centre at Bellarmine University in Louisville, Kentucky, number more than 10,000. The Centre has now grown to far in excess of 50,000 items, including Merton's original manuscripts, photographs, recordings and calligraphies.

Letter-writing was an apostolate of friendship for Merton, a way to engage in the issues of the day with intellectuals, popes, bishops, politicians, jazz musicians, poets and students from other parts of the world. There is an intimacy about these letters. Merton writes with much more freedom in his letters than he does in his published books, which were always subject to the scrutiny of his superiors.

Merton's journals were published by Harper, San Francisco, in seven volumes in 1993, twenty-five years after his death. They reveal a very human, very fallible man writing down thoughts that soared into the heavens but also trudged through desolate lands of doubt and self-recrimination. Dissatisfaction with himself and his present knowledge, and with Western culture's proposed easy answers to the problems facing the world was the fuel that kept his spiritual life on fire, kept him searching for God. For Merton, mere complacency and settling for the easiest solutions were the greatest enemies of a sincere spiritual life.

## What others said of Merton

Fr Matthew, who joined the community at Gethsemani in June 1960 and completed his novitiate under Merton:

> He was humble, gentle and obedient. But he could be British. The British have a capacity for cutting you down, but they do it with style. He could do that, not very often, but he could do it. He was witty in a British way – it was a bright humour – He was very creative. He had a new idea every month for some project or another … The monks made nothing of him because he didn't make anything of himself. He was not our famous writer and poet – or our holy mystic. He was just one of the boys.

Daniel Berrigan SJ:

> He was totally unselfconscious about anything like fame. He was very much himself – plain-spoken, warm-hearted, open to friendship, and very modest about his attainment.

Lawrence Cunningham, professor of theology at Notre Dame University:

> Merton was a mercurial kind of person … In the late 1950s he had this idea of going to Latin America and having a hermitage, or a small simple monastery … That was a crazy idea. This was a guy who couldn't drive a car … he was hopeless at organization.

John Eudes Bamberger, a Gethsemani monk:

> It was Merton's enthusiasm for the spiritual life that marked his teaching. He had that kind of enthusiasm with no airs and graces at all … All the young monks liked Merton … he took his preparation or class very seriously. He always had more notes than he could deliver … He always spoke with great personal investment, with a lot of spontaneity, and with

emotional involvement which made his classes interesting and highly personal ... He taught us how to retain our humanity, our humanness ...

... I remember him saying,

You come to the monastery and, after a few months, or half a year or so, you think, 'Oh, this is difficult', and then after a year or so more, you think, 'Oh, this is very difficult', and then another year or so, you think, 'This is impossible!' So that's the way it should be. You just find that, if you have to do it yourself, the monastic life is impossible. You have to surrender to the monastic discipline and just trust that it will work out.

Finally, Merton warned the scholastics: 'Don't build your life on a mud pile like me. Be a disciple of Jesus Christ.'

## Reflection

O Lord God, I have no idea where I am going. I do not see the road ahead of me. I cannot know for certain where it will end. Nor do I really know myself and the fact that I think I am following Your will does not mean that I am actually doing so. But I believe the desire to please You does in fact please You. And I hope that I have that desire in all that I am doing. I hope that I will never to anything apart from that desire to please You. And I know that if I do this You will lead me by the right road, though I may know nothing about it. Therefore, I will trust You always though I may seem to be lost and in the shadow of death. I will not fear for You are ever with me, and You will never leave me to make my journey alone.

# CHAPTER FIVE

# Pope Paul VI
## (1897–1978)

## Childhood

Giovanni Battista Montini was born on 26 September 1897 in the village of Concesio, in the province of Brescia, Lombardy, where the family country house was situated. His father, Giorgio Montini, was a lawyer, journalist and a member of the Italian Parliament. His mother, Giudetta Alghisi, was from a family of rural nobility. Giovanni was farmed out to a local wet nurse, a thirty-year-old peasant woman with four children of her own, and he spent the first fourteen months of his life in a rustic cottage halfway up a hillside.

In 1903, Giovanni (or Battista as he was known to his family and friends) started primary school at the Jesuit Collegio Cesare Arici. He was a 'spirited' child and was asked to sit in the front so that he could be supervised more closely! His mother read to him in French, a language with which he was at ease from an early age. As a teenager, he had a passion for cycling.

In 1914, Battista's parents decided that he should leave the Jesuit College of Arici for health reasons (he suffered from a rather serious cardiac imbalance) and finish his education privately, taking his exams at the state high school. He later confessed that long periods of enforced solitude were more fruitful that any regular course of study.

## Seminary

In May 1915, Italy was at war with Austria, whose border was only forty miles from Brescia. Battista thought that he might become a Benedictine monk in the monastery at Chiari but the abbot dissuaded him on the grounds that he would not have the physical strength to cope with the rigours of monastic life. Instead, in October 1915, Battista 'entered the seminary' in Brescia. By special dispensation from Bishop Giacino Gaggia, he became an external student allowed to live and study at home. At that time, the regular seminary of Sant'Angelo was being used as a storehouse for a military hospital.

Battista was ordained priest on Saturday, 19 May 1920, along with fourteen other seminarians. He was only twenty-two when he was ordained. He proposed to do further studies in literature at the Sapienza University in Rome, after which he would do a doctorate in history.

## Rome and abroad

In Rome, he lived initially at the Lombardy College. Very soon, however, he was summoned by Monsignor Giuseppe Pizzardo from the Vatican and was told that he was to enter the Academy for Noble Ecclesiastics and would study canon law. To this day, the Academy is the residence for the training of future Church diplomats and papal nuncios. Battista studied canon law at the Gregorian University, while living at the Academy. He was mistrustful of the Academy from the beginning, feeling, as he did, that its natural pathway was one of ambition and the seeking of honours.

In 1922, Battista had his first experience of being abroad. He was sent to Austria and Germany. He was supposed to learn German but found the language 'every day more convoluted and incomprehensible'. He called on Eugenio Pacelli (the future Pope Pius XII), Papal Nuncio in Munich. Suddenly, he received an order from Monsignor Pizzardo to 'get his canon law studies over as soon as possible'. Battista returned to Rome and to the Gregorian University where he was exempted from some subjects. He was awarded his doctoral degree in canon law on 9 December 1922.

On 4 January 1923, Battista received yet another order from Monsignor Pizzardo, telling him to 'hold himself ready' to enter the Vatican Secretariat of State. By June 1923, he was on his way to Poland to work in the nunciature in Warsaw. He wrote to a friend: 'Morally, this is a trial, just office routine and professionally tedious.' He had problems with the Polish language, calling it 'questa dannata lingua' – 'this damned language'. On 2 October 1923, he received a telegram from the Vatican Secretary of State, Cardinal Pietro Gaspari. It read: 'Montini authorised return Rome.'

Montini had to wait until 20 January 1924 for an audience with Pope Pius XI. In the meantime, his immediate superior, Monsignor Pizzardo, told him that the Pope had named him 'ecclesiastical assistant' (chaplain) to the Catholic students of Rome. On 9 August, he got a letter from

Pizzardo that decided his future: from October he would enter the Secretariat of State as an *addetto*, little more than a glorified office boy. In April 1925 he became a 'domestic prelate' – a monsignor – assigned to the 'second section' of the Secretariat, which dealt with foreign governments.

Montini was still involved with the students of Rome. He prepared lectures for the students and devoured Tübingen Professor Karl Adam's *The Essence of Catholicism*, which left a permanent mark on his own theology of the Church (ecclesiology). The book was later censored. The Church to which Montini introduced his students was in need of reform. He found this theme in Karl Adam. This is why the Holy Office (today known as the Congregation for the Doctrine of the Faith) 'censured' Adam's book, that is, had it withdrawn from Roman bookshops. Montini got hold of the remaining copies and handed them out to his trusted friends.

In November 1925, Montini took charge of the Catholic Student Movement throughout Italy. Thus, at the age of twenty-eight, he became the covert leader of the intellectual opposition to the Italian Fascists under Benito Mussolini. With study went works of charity. He accompanied the students in the work of the St Vincent de Paul in the poverty-stricken quarters of Rome.

The Fascist press began to attack Montini by name. They accused him of being a 'meddler in politics'. On 29 May 1931, all Catholic student movements in Italy were dissolved. The Roman offices were raided while Montini read his breviary in his office. He was dismissed from the post of national chaplain of the Catholic Students (FUCI).

Pope Pius XI wrote in his correspondence: 'Monsignor Montini has gifts destined to permit him to render services to the Church on a much higher level.' Montini was actually overawed by Pius XI, who always made him think of the *Dies Irae* (the Day of Wrath/Anger) – Pius was often fussy and given to uncontrollable rages.

Montini found the whole Vatican Curial style 'too grand', producing people 'incapable of dealing with ordinary everyday life'. His heart was somewhere other than working in the Secretariat. His isolation was enhanced by the fact that he now lived inside the Vatican, although he managed to stay in touch with life outside. He took seriously his teaching of Church history at the Pontifical Academy. In 1935–36, his lectures were on the Lutheran and Anglican Reformations.

By 1937, Montini was seeing the Secretary of State, Cardinal Eugenio Pacelli, every morning. He also got to know Pius XI better, finding him 'always very friendly and most clear-minded'. On 13 December 1937,

Montini was appointed 'substitute' at the Secretariat of State. At forty, he was now, in effect, the chief executive officer to Cardinal Pacelli. A new apartment went with the job – this time in the Apostolic Palace, the papal residence itself. Montini would remain there for the next seventeen years. It was his longest stay in any one place.

## Outbreak of war

Montini was the first to be called to the deathbed of Pius XI at 4.00 am on 10 February 1939. On 1 March 1939, Cardinal Eugenio Pacelli was elected as Pius XII. Within two weeks, Adolf Hitler had annexed Bohemia and Moravia. With the outbreak of the Second World War the objective of Vatican policy was to prevent Italy joining the hostilities on the German side.

The invasion of Holland, Belgium and Luxembourg on 10 May 1940 called out for a condemnation from the Vatican. Pius XII confided in Montini:

> We would like to utter words of fire against such actions; and the only thing that restrains us from speaking is the fear of making the plight of victims worse.

Italy declared war on France and Britain on 10 June 1940. In the spring of 1941, Italy had lost Eritrea, Somalia and Ethiopia and their army of 250,000 had surrendered to the British.

In July 1943, the British and Americans invaded Sicily. Part of the plan was that 500 American bombers would attack Rome. On 19 July 1943, Rome was bombed and hundreds of citizens were killed. Pope Pius XII went to the shattered Basilica of San Lorenzo that afternoon, accompanied by Montini, and stayed for two and a half hours. It was the first time the Pope had been outside the Vatican since 1940. He knelt among the ruins and recited the *De Profundis* ('Out of the Depths ... '). Rome was bombed again on 13 August and Pius was once again first on the scene with Montini.

German troops occupied Rome on 9 September 1943. The Jews of Rome began to be rounded up on 16 October 1943. Two thousand nine hundred Roman Jews perished in the concentration camps, along with some 6,000 Jews from other parts of Italy.

Rome was eventually liberated by the Allies on 4 June 1944. Half a million Romans walked to St Peter's Square and cheered *'Viva il Papà'*. Pius was acclaimed as *Defensor Civitatis* (Defender of the City). Montini learned of Mussolini's death on 28 April 1945. Hitler committed suicide on 30 April. VE Day came on 8 May.

## The post-war years

In the immediate post-war years, ecumenism and religious liberty were anathema to the Holy Office as long as Cardinal Alfredo Ottaviani (1890–1979) was in charge. Montini had been a consultor to the Holy Office since 1937 but was powerless to influence its decisions.

The late 1940s and early 1950s were the years of the 'new theology' (*la nouvelle théologie*) developed by French Dominicans like Marie-Dominique Chenu and Yves Congar, and French Jesuits like Jean Daniélou and Henri de Lubac. Montini read these theologians with avid interest. The 'new theology' took the form of retrieving elements of the neglected heritage of the Early Fathers of the Church, with reference to contemporary social problems. The 'new theology' movement was also known as the *ressourcement* (back to the sources) project. In the 1940s the *ressourcement* theologians came under heavy criticism from the proponents of Strict Observance Thomism (the theology of Thomas Aquinas). The charge was that they were heading into the dangerous territory of Modernism (already mentioned in Chapter 3).

On 12 August 1950, Pius XII's encyclical *Humani Generis* was devoted to the topic of 'new theological opinions threatening to undermine the foundations of Catholic doctrine'. Although the *ressourcement* theologians were never named the encyclical was widely interpreted as referring to their project. Anonymity meant that everyone was under suspicion. The encyclical was followed by 'disciplinary measures', which threw many of the French theologians out of their professorial posts and, in some cases, exiled them. It was the most drastic and embarrassing action of Pius XII's pontificate.

Of all the French theologians silenced by *Humani Generis* the Jesuit Henri de Lubac was the closest spiritually to Montini. De Lubac's response to his silencing was magnificent. He wrote *Meditation on the Church* (1953) in which he demonstrated his great love for the Church. This book was a favourite of Montini's. It made a deep impression, not only because of its vast patristic learning but, above all, because of its deep *sensus ecclesiae* – 'feel for the Church'.

During his nineteen-year pontificate (1939–58), Pius XII held only two consistories – in 1946 and 1953. He did not create Montini a cardinal in

1953. Instead, he appointed him Archbishop of Milan and told the people of Milan that he was sending Montini to them as his 'personal gift'.

## Archbishop of Milan

Montini was ordained bishop in St Peter's on 12 December 1954 by Cardinal Eugene Tisserant, Dean of the Sacred College, standing in for Pius XII who was ill in bed, and delivered an address about Montini's appointment from his sickbed over radio to those assembled in St Peter's Basilica. Montini felt overwhelmed by the immensity of the task that lay before him in Milan. The move to the pastoral care of the Milan archdiocese, with its 1,000 churches, 2,500 priests and 3,500,000 parishioners, was distinctly alarming.

On 5 January 1955, Montini formally took possession of the Cathedral of Milan. From the outset, he was determined to reach out to the Milanese working class. He wanted to show 'the Church's love for those who were estranged from her'. He put on a hard hat, went down mines, visited factories, toured Communist districts never penetrated by his predecessor, Cardinal Schuster. Montini took with him a portable Mass kit which he set up and used wherever possible. His goal was the re-introduction of the faith to a city without much religion. 'If only we can say Our Father and know what it means, then we would understand the Christian faith.'

Montini became a great builder of churches. He increased the number in the diocese by more than 10 per cent. He took immense trouble over his sermons, especially for the great feasts when the cathedral was crowded. He never recycled old material – his sermons flowed from his prayer and his reading.

By the time Pius XII died on 9 October 1958, there were only fifty-one cardinals, half of whom were over eighty. Cardinal Angelo Roncalli, Patriarch of Venice, is quoted as saying at the time: 'If Montini were a cardinal, I would have no hesitation in voting for him.'

The election of Cardinal Roncalli as Pope John XXIII on 28 October changed Montini's life. Not only was he almost immediately created a cardinal on 19 November 1958 – that should have happened four years earlier – but he became the leading candidate for the papal succession. John XXIII appointed Montini to several Vatican congregations, which resulted in many visits to Rome in the coming years.

To everyone's surprise, Pope John announced the calling of an Ecumenical Council on 25 January 1959. Montini prepared for the Council by composing lectures and pastoral letters in close collaboration with Monsignor Carlo Colombo, from now on his chief theological adviser, whom he would later appoint to be his successor in Milan. On 6 November 1961, Montini was appointed to the Central Preparatory Commission of the Second Vatican Council. In the interim, with John XXIII's encouragement, he had spent a month in the US and in Brazil in 1960. In Brazil, he met the famous Archbishop Hélder Câmara of Recife. In the US he took fourteen flights in thirteen days. He received an honorary doctorate along with President Dwight Eisenhower at Notre Dame University. In 1962 he journeyed to Africa ,where he visited Ghana, Sudan, Kenya, Congo, Zimbabwe, South Africa and Nigeria. These visits ensured that Montini's name became known in a wider Church.

Montini expected the Council to deal with collegiality in the Church, the relationship between the pope and bishops. He defended the idea that the liturgy should be in the vernacular and insisted that the Chrism Mass (when the Holy Oils are blessed) on Holy Thursday should be a concelebration of the local diocesan bishop with his priests.

On 21 September 1962, Pope John XXIII learned that he had cancer and that, consequently, he had not long to live. Montini was proposing that there should be three sessions of the Council – John XXIII thought that it would all be over by Christmas! By proposing three sessions, Montini was, in effect, raising the question of the papal succession.

## Pope Paul VI

The Second Vatican Council opened on 11 October 1962. The First Session lasted two crowded months, at the end of which no decrees had been passed. Pope John died on 3 June 1963. The conclave to elect his successor would be the biggest ever. In 1958, a mere fifty-one cardinals assembled to elect John XXIII. In 1963, eighty-one cardinals were eligible to vote. On 21 June 1963, Cardinal Montini was elected on the sixth ballot. He chose to take the name 'Paul', explaining afterwards that he wanted to reach out to the modern Gentiles.

Pope Paul VI spent the summer at the papal residence of Castelgandolfo. During this time he wrote in his spiritual diary:

The colloquy with God must be full and endless … The position is unique. It brings great solitude. I was solitary before, but now my solitude becomes complete and awesome.

He knew only too well his great need of personal prayer if he was to fulfil this onerous mission. Someone in whom Pope Paul did confide on a regular basis was his Jesuit confessor, Fr Paolo Dezza, who was delivered by car to the Vatican every Friday evening at 7.00 pm. The only thing Fr Dezza ever revealed about the experience was that Paul VI was 'a man of great joy.'

Pope Paul reopened the Vatican Council on 29 September 1963, giving it four key priorities: 1) A better understanding of the Catholic Church; 2) Church reforms; 3) Advancing the unity of Christianity; 4) Dialogue with the world. Compared to John XXIII he generally had a 'hands-off' approach as regards the day-to-day running of the Council. He preferred to work quietly, receiving daily written reports on the most important events from his private secretary, Monsignor Pasquale Macchi.

## Travels abroad and ecumenical contacts

Pope Paul went to the Holy Land in 1964 to meet the Ecumenical Patriarch of Constantinople, Athnenagoras I, leader of the Greek Orthodox Church. The meeting took place in the Church of the Holy Sepulchre in Jerusalem. This was the first ever meeting between an Orthodox patriarch and a pope since the schism between the two churches in 1054. Paul was the first pope in centuries to meet the heads of various Eastern Orthodox faiths. He labelled the Eastern Churches 'sister Churches'. The last pope who planned to go to the Holy Land was Innocent III (1198–1216), who wanted to carry out a decision of the Fourth Lateran Council (1215) by leading a Crusade against the Saracens!

Paul VI was the last pope to be crowned with the papal tiara. On 13 November 1964, at the end of the Second Session of the Vatican Council, Paul laid his tiara on the altar of St Peter's as a symbolic gift to the world's poor and as a sign of the renunciation of human glory and power in keeping with the renewed spirit of the Council. It was announced that the tiara would be sold and the money obtained given to charity. The purchasers arranged for the tiara to be displayed as a gift to American Catholics in the crypt of the Basilica of the National Shrine of the Immaculate Conception in Washington, DC.

On 9 April 1964, it was announced, without previous warning, that Paul had founded a Secretariat for Non-Christians. Its purpose was 'to study atheism and unbelief'. It was later renamed the Pontifical Council for Interreligious Dialogue, and a year later became the Pontifical Council for

Dialogue with Non-Believers. On 14 September 1965, Paul set up the Synod of Bishops, to be chosen from the greater part of the episcopal conferences, and to be convened by the pope for consultation and collaboration when this seems most opportune for the general good of the Church. Several meetings were held on specific issues during his pontificate, such as the Synod of Bishops on evangelisation in the modern world, which started on 9 September 1974.

On 2 November 1964, Paul went to India, and on the next day, the Feast of St Francis Xavier, he ordained bishops from all five continents. To make the point that Christianity was indigenous in India, Paul became the first pope to preside at a Mass in the Syro-Malankara Rite. He participated in the Eucharistic Congress in Bombay.

On 4 October 1965, the Feast of Francis of Assisi, Paul spoke in French at the United Nations in New York. The most famous phrase from his speech was, '*Jamais plus la guerre! Jamais plus la guerre!*' ('Never war again!'). As a gesture of good will, Paul gave to the UN two pieces of papal jewellery, a diamond cross and ring, with the hopes that the proceeds from their sale at auction would contribute to the UN's efforts to end human suffering. To foster this good will he decreed an annual peace day to be celebrated on 1 January every year.

On 7 December 1965, there was the common declaration of the 'lifting of the anathemas' of 1054 between the Roman Catholic and Greek Orthodox Churches. This lifting of the excommunications paved the way for Paul's historic visit to Constantinople (Istanbul) in 1967.

On 23–24 March 1966, the Primate of the Anglican Church and Archbishop of Canterbury, Michael Ramsey, came to the Vatican and was welcomed in the Sistine Chapel. Archbishop Ramsey met Paul three times during his visit and opened the Anglican Centre in Rome to increase their mutual understanding. Pope Paul gave Archbishop Ramsey a ring after a service in the Basilica of St Paul's Outside-the-Walls. Pope Paul was often a master of the symbolic. He described the Anglican Church as 'our beloved sister Church'. This description was unique to Paul and was not used by later popes.

In 1967, Pope Paul visited the shrine of Our Lady of Fátima in Portugal on the fiftieth anniversary of the apparitions there. He made a pastoral visit to Uganda in 1969, the first by a reigning pope to Africa.

Paul VI authored seven encyclicals in the earlier years of his pontificate – encyclicals on the Church, the Virgin Mary, the mystery of faith, social teaching and the celibate priesthood. His best known encyclical was

*Humanae Vitae* (*Of Human Life*, subtitled *On the Regulation of Birth*), published on 25 July 1968. In this encyclical Pope Paul reaffirmed the Catholic Church's traditional view of marriage and marital relations and its condemnation of artificial birth control. He was concerned but not surprised by the negative reaction in Western Europe and the US to the encyclical. While most regions and bishops supported him, a small but important part of them, especially in the Netherlands, Canada and Germany, openly disagreed with him, which wounded him deeply for the rest of his life. Paul famously remarked, 'in twenty years' time they'll call me a prophet'. He never wrote another encyclical after *Humanae Vitae*, even though he reigned for another ten years.

Shortly after arriving at the airport in Manila, the Philippines, on 27 November 1970, Pope Paul was the target of an assassination attempt. The would-be assassin, Benjamin Mendoza y Amor Flores of La Paz, Bolivia, was subdued by the Pope's personal bodyguard and travel organiser, Monsignor Paul Marcinkus.

Pope Paul VI held six consistories between 1965 and 1977, which raised 143 men to the cardinalate in his fifteen years as pope. The next three popes were created cardinals by him. The six consistories made the College of Cardinals more international, with an increased number of cardinals from the Developing World.

## Final days

On 16 March 1978, former Italian prime minister Aldo Moro – a friend of Paul VI's from his student days – was kidnapped by a far-left Italian terrorist group known as the Red Brigades – this group hoped that their comrades would soon be released from jail as part of a deal to save Moro's life. Italian Prime Minister Giulio Andreotti was adamant: no deals, no amnesty, no exile. The consequences would be too grave.

On 20 April, Moro appealed directly to Paul to intervene. On the same day, Paul had already written a letter to the Red Brigades:

On my knees I beg you, free Aldo Moro, simply and without conditions …
Men of the Red Brigades, leave me … the hope that in your heart feelings of humanity will triumph. In prayer and always loving you I await proof of that.

On 9 May, the bullet-riddled body of Aldo Moro, leader of the Christian Democrats, was found in the boot of a red Renault car in Rome. On receiving the dreadful news, Paul retired to his private chapel to be alone and pray. There was a special memorial service in St John Lateran, Rome's cathedral. The Moro family absented themselves from the service. If they had gone along they would have heard Paul upbraid God for allowing this appalling deed to happen. Paul spoke for the nation, the *patria*.

The feast of Saints Peter and Paul, 29 June, was the fifteenth anniversary of Paul's coronation. He used the occasion to sum up and say farewell:

> I have kept the faith ... That was my duty ... to be faithful. I've done everything. Now I've finished ... Lord, to whom shall we go? You have the words of eternal life.

At the Angelus on Sunday, 9 July, Paul said his farewell to the city of Rome. He left the Vatican to go to the papal summer residence, Castelgandolfo. On Sunday, 6 August, the Feast of the Transfiguration, Paul was confined to bed on the orders of his doctors. From his bed he participated in Sunday Mass at 18.00. Towards the end of Mass, he had a massive heart attack, lingered for another three hours and then, at 21.41, he died. According to the terms of his will, he was buried in the 'true earth' and he does not therefore have an ornate tomb but is buried in a grave beneath the floor of St Peter's Basilica, in the area of the basilica's crypt near the tombs of other popes.

Pope Paul's Jesuit confessor, Fr Paolo Dezza, said that 'this Pope is a man of great joy'. After Paul's death, he is reported to have said:

> If Paul VI was not a saint when he was elected Pope, he became one during his pontificate. I was able to witness not only with what energy and dedication he toiled for Christ and the Church but also and above all, how much he suffered for Christ and the Church. I always admired not only his deep inner resignation but also his constant abandonment to divine providence.

The diocesan process for the beatification of Paul VI opened in Rome on 11 May 1993 under Pope John Paul II. On 20 December 2012, Benedict XVI declared that the late Pope had lived a life of heroic virtue, which meant that he could be called 'Venerable'. On 12 December 2013, Vatican officials, comprising a medical panel, approved a supposed miracle that was attributed to the intercession of the late pontiff, which was the curing of an unborn child in California in the 1990s. Paul was beatified on 19 October 2014.

The second miracle required for his canonisation was reported to have occurred in Verona in 2014. It also involved the healing of an unborn child. Theologians, advising the Congregation for the Causes of Saints, voiced their approval to this miracle on 13 December 2017 (following the confirmation of doctors on 26 October). Paul VI was canonised on 14 October 2018, along with the martyred Archbishop Oscar Romero of El Salvador.

## Reflection

Either tacitly or aloud – but always forcefully – we are being asked: 'Do you really believe what you are proclaiming? Do you live what you believe? Do you really preach what you live?' The witness of life has become more than ever an essential condition for real effectiveness in preaching. (*Evangelization in the Modern World*, 76)

# CHAPTER SIX

# Dorothy Day
(1897–1980)

## Childhood

Dorothy Day was born in Brooklyn, New York, on 8 November 1897, into a lower-middle-class family. She had three brothers and one sister. Her father, John, was an itinerant sportswriter. The name of God was never mentioned in the family. Her mother, Grace, and her father never went to church; none of the children were baptised. The family were living in San Francisco until the earthquake of 1906. Dorothy remembered that the earthquake lasted for two minutes and twenty seconds. What she remembered most plainly about the earthquake was the human warmth and kindness of everyone afterwards. For days, people poured out of burning San Francisco and, while the crisis lasted, people loved each other. The Day family lost everything in the earthquake and they moved to Chicago, where they settled.

It was the first time that the family was really poor. They lived in an apartment over a store. In Chicago, Dorothy met her first Catholic. Further up from their apartment was a Mrs Barrett and six little Barretts. It was Mrs Barrett who gave Dorothy her first impulse towards Catholicism. One day, Dorothy burst into Mrs Barrett's bedroom and found her on her knees, saying her prayers. Dorothy suddenly felt a warm burst of love toward Mrs Barrett that she never forgot, a feeling of gratitude and happiness that continued to warm her heart when she remembered her. Dorothy felt that Mrs Barrett 'had God and there was beauty and joy in her life'.

## University of Illinois

Dorothy was baptised in the Episcopal Church as a youth but her interest in religion soon faded. At the age of sixteen, she won a $300 scholarship to the University of Illinois, sponsored by Hearst newspapers. The examination consisted of a test in Greek and Latin. One day, in class, a professor whom she admired made a statement that she always remembered – that religion was something that had brought great comfort to people throughout the ages, so we ought not to criticise it.

In 1914, as a freshman at the University of Illinois, she joined the Socialist Party, but it was mostly a symbolic gesture. After two years at the university, she chose to dispense with formal education altogether and set off eagerly for New York.

## The Bohemian journalist

Dorothy got a job with the *New York Call*, a paper of socialists, trade unionists and anarchists. Amongst those she interviewed was Leon Trotsky. On 21 March 1917, Dorothy joined the crowds in Madison Square Garden gathered to celebrate the February Revolution in Russia and the overthrow of the Tsar.

On 10 November 1917, two days after her twentieth birthday, Dorothy, together with forty-eight other women, was arrested in a Suffragist picket line. Worse was to follow. On 15 November, the 'Night of Terror', as it came to be known, there was a brutal incident. About forty guards, all armed with clubs, dragged, kicked, trampled and choked the women. Three guards attacked Dorothy so violently the story made the newspapers. They throttled her, held her arms above her head, and smashed her head several times against an iron bench, almost beating her senseless. Later, she participated in a seven-day hunger strike. She wept throughout the week while reading the Psalms. Women finally succeeded in getting the vote in 1920.

In New York, Dorothy soon fell in with a circle of bohemians and rebels, the 'Village Set', who congregated about the Provincetown Playhouse. During the cold winter of 1917–18, she was the inseparable companion of the playwright Eugene O'Neill, or Gene as she used to call him. Often, after listening to one of O'Neill's gloomy monologues, Dorothy would guide him home and put him to bed, and then, in the first hours of dawn, drop into a back pew of St Joseph's Catholic Church on Sixth Avenue.

One evening, an old friend of Gene's, Louis Holliday, brought some heroin from a waiter in an Italian restaurant. Louis later died in Dorothy's arms. The incident prompted Dorothy to break loose from this sad, careless social circle. She began training to be a nurse at King's Hospital in

Brooklyn in early 1918. This was the time of the Spanish flu. The worst of the flu had abated by November.

## Dorothy in love

In November 1918, Dorothy met Lionel Moise, a newspaper man, and fell hopelessly in love with him. Lionel was considered to be a brilliant reporter and became a legend in city newsrooms across the country. Lionel was teaching Dorothy how to write as a journalist. When she became pregnant Lionel abandoned her, saying, 'I feel sorry for you but I'm still going to Chicago', where he had secured a new job.

Dorothy, hoping to forestall her abandonment by Lionel, chose to have an abortion. It was a futile gesture, and the memory of this waste of life would remain with her always. The abortion left Dorothy ill and traumatised. Sometime in early 1920, heartbroken and suffering complications from the abortion, she returned to Greenwich Village. There it seems that she tried to commit suicide twice, once by overdosing on laudanum and another with a gas oven, but in each instance she was saved by friends.

## A brief marriage

In the spring of 1920, Dorothy met Berkeley Tobey. On a train to Connecticut he said to her, 'Let's get married.' He was wealthy, had plenty of ideas and no need to work. They got married in Connecticut in 1920. She was twenty-two, he was thirty-nine. They travelled in Europe and Dorothy worked on a novel in Capri and the Bay of Naples. There she was, married to a man she did not love, writing about the man she did (Lionel). 'I married on the rebound ... I married him for his money.' When they returned to New York in April 1921 the marriage was dissolved and Dorothy rarely spoke of Berkeley again.

## A victim of Red hysteria

In 1922, Dorothy was living in Chicago, working on *The Liberator*, a Communist journal. She was arrested for being the inmate of a disorderly house. While in jail for a few days, she was to have a solitary taste of injustice that set her squarely on the side of revolution. She described herself as the 'victim of Red hysteria' in America – the fear of Communism. She recalled being searched for drugs, stripped naked, given prison clothes and put in a cell. In the cell next to hers there was a drug addict who beat her head against the walls of her cell and howled like a wild animal. Dorothy wrote afterwards: 'I have never heard such anguish, such unspeakable suffering' (*Selected Writings*, p.19).

The years that followed were marked by loneliness and restless searching. In the spring of 1924, Dorothy published a frankly autobiographical novel, *The Eleventh Virgin,* which she later described as 'a very bad book'. Whatever the merits of the work, the proceeds of the sale of the movie rights enabled her to buy her first home for $1,200, a cottage on a beach on Staten Island in a colony of artists and radicals. With this move began a period that would later stand out in her memory as a time of 'natural happiness'.

## Staten Island – Forster Batterham – Catholicism

Once Dorothy moved to Staten Island, her friends began to follow her. Among her new friends was one Forster Batterham. He had studied biology at the universities of Virginia and Georgia. Influenced by Forster, the soil around the cottage became holy for Dorothy. Forster dragged her away from her books to go for long walks along the beach, examining mussel larvae along the way. They also shared a love of opera.

Dorothy wrote of Forster: 'The man I loved ... was an anarchist, an Englishman by descent and a biologist.' They fished in the bay, studied the stars, and collected specimens on the beach. Little by little, a whole new world opened up for Dorothy. She became an indefatigable novel reader and spent the first few winters on the beach, reading Tolstoy, Dostoevsky and Dickens. She began to read the Bible and *The Imitation of Christ* and she felt in herself a great desire to pray.

Dorothy began to pray daily. She tells us that she began to pray because she had to. Over and over in her mind she kept hearing the phrase 'Religion is the opiate of the people', yet, as she walked along the beach, she felt it appropriate to say the *Te Deum* (a hymn of praise to God), which she had learned in the Episcopal Church. When she was walking around the house, she found herself addressing the Blessed Virgin and turning up at Mass regularly on Sunday mornings.

Forster found all talk of religion incomprehensible and distressing. He was a rationalist, delighted by nature, but scornful of humankind and the injustice of human institutions. He was full of anger at Dorothy's absorption in the supernatural rather than the natural, the unseen rather than the seen. Dorothy did not share his pessimism or extreme individualism.

Ironically, Forster's ardent love of creation brought Dorothy closer to the Creator of all things.

## Tamar Teresa

By June 1925, Dorothy knew that she was pregnant again! In her joy and gratitude her first thoughts were of God. She was determined to have the child baptised a Catholic, cost what it might. Tamar Teresa was born on 4 March 1926. Tamar is the Hebrew word for palm tree and Dorothy chose Teresa after St Teresa of Avila, whose autobiography she had been reading. On 3 July, Tamar was baptised a Catholic. Forster caught lobster for the celebration but left in the middle of it, silent and angry.

Meanwhile, a certain Sister Aloysia, whom Dorothy had met quite by chance while walking on the beach, came to give her catechism lessons three times a week. Forster would have nothing to do with the Catholic Church, or with Dorothy if she were part of it. A tense period between them ensued. Forster would not talk about the faith and relapsed into complete silence if Dorothy tried to bring up the subject. An anarchist and an atheist, he was averse to any ceremony before officials of either Church or state. It was killing Dorothy to think of leaving him.

Nevertheless, on 29 December 1927, Dorothy was baptised conditionally, since she had already been baptised in the Episcopal Church. Sister Aloysia acted as godparent. Dorothy made her first confession immediately afterwards and received Communion the next morning. In one of her letters to Forster, written in the months after her Catholic baptism, Dorothy wrote: 'I do love you more than anything in the world, but I cannot help my religious sense, which tortures me unless I do what I believe right.' Despite their differences, Dorothy remained a friend of Forster's for the rest of her life.

Dorothy tells us herself that she had no particular joy in partaking of the three sacraments of Baptism, Penance and Eucharist. She certainly had no consolation. Rather, she felt like a hypocrite. Here she was writing against capitalism and imperialism and this was like going over to the opposition, because, of course, the Church was aligned with property, with the wealthy, with the state, with capitalism. She wrote: 'I loved the Church for Christ made visible. Not for itself, because it was so often a scandal to me.'

Dorothy never regretted for one minute the step she had taken in becoming a Catholic, but for a whole year there was little joy for her. She was confirmed on the Feast of Pentecost in 1929, which she described as a joyous affair. She took the names Maria Teresa.

In the meantime Dorothy and Tamar travelled out to California and Mexico, and then shuttled between Staten Island and Florida. They lived in Mexico for six months until June 1930. That autumn they returned to Staten Island. Dorothy kept writing articles, short stories and novel after novel (never published), seeking freelance work, a success here and there from *Commonweal*, a Catholic publication, and the *New Masses*, a Communist one. As an adult, Tamar had given up trying to keep the chronology of their whereabouts, and the addresses of all the apartments they lived in blurred together, but all these moves were hard on her. It was Staten Island that Tamar and Dorothy both loved and returned to.

## Peter Maurin

In December 1932 there was a hunger march planned for Washington DC. Dorothy decided to cover the march for *Commonweal* and the Jesuit publication *America*. The Depression was worsening and farmers had come from all over the country to ask for a moratorium on evictions and forced sales, and for the cancellation of mortgages and seed loans.

After the march Dorothy visited the Shrine of the Immaculate Conception on the Feast of the Immaculate Conception, 8 December. This visit would become much treasured by her as a time when one of her most profound prayers was heard. She was on the brink of losing her faith in the face of the Church's indifference to what called to her most deeply – compassion for the downtrodden. Dorothy found herself praying to the Blessed Mother: 'Here I am – what would you have me do?'

When she returned to New York, she found, waiting at her door, Peter Maurin, a short, somewhat unkempt man with a thick French accent and fire in his eyes. Peter's spirit and ideas would dominate the rest of Dorothy's life.

Peter Maurin was born in 1877 in the ancient Languedoc region of southern France. He was one of twenty-one children born to a peasant family. He sailed for America in 1909. For the next twenty years he drifted through the east and Midwest, performing various kinds of manual labour. Believing that work should be regarded as a gift, he was happy to offer his labour in exchange for room and board. He liked to consider himself a troubadour of Christ, a type of St Francis of Assisi. What little money he earned was spent either on books or given away to those in greater need.

Peter introduced Dorothy to the social teachings of the Church. He introduced her to current Catholic thinkers like Romano Guardini, G. K. Chesterton and Hilaire Belloc. He also spoke of Francis of Assisi and the modern Desert Father, Charles de Foucauld. Peter had one ambition – to change the hearts and minds of people and give them a vision of a world where it was easier to be good. He spoke of farming communes, or 'agronomic universities', where there would be cottage industry and cooperatives.

Peter wanted Dorothy to follow in the footsteps of St Catherine of Siena and advise the popes! 'Let's start a newspaper,' is what Dorothy heard him say. He had in mind broadsheets and pamphlets that he could hand out while talking in Union Square.

## The Catholic Worker

On 1 May 1933, the worst year of the Depression, during the May Day demonstrations in Union Square, copies of the first edition of the *Catholic Worker* were sold for a penny a copy. Dorothy wanted to report things as they were in order to arouse the conscience of the people. She had begun and could not be stopped, and so the paper became hers alone. Peter took no further part in it except to submit a handful of essays for each issue,

The growth of the paper was phenomenal. From its first run of 2,500, circulation had reached 20,000 four months later. Dorothy reported on the strikes, affecting thousands, that were covering the country. She wanted a paper for blacks and whites but written by both, to impress upon her readers that the paper was for all workers. By the sixth issue, Dorothy was tackling Hitler's persecution of the Jews and anti-Semitism, not only in Germany but also in the US. By May Day 1934 100,000 copies were being printed – distributed in Madison Square and Columbus Circle. People of all nationalities approached *Catholic Worker* volunteers, asking for copies.

Within two years circulation had increased to 150,000. Seminaries and churches around the country ordered bundles. Quite soon a staff of ardent volunteers began to congregate around the newspaper office, a former barbershop, on the ground floor of Dorothy's 15th Street apartment.

Meanwhile, Peter Maurin had written a letter to all the bishops of the country urging the establishment of houses of hospitality in their dioceses. Homeless men and women began arriving at the door in New York, asking where to find these houses described in the newspaper. Dorothy's response was to rent an apartment. Other apartments were soon needed, and before long the *Catholic Worker* occupied its own building on Charles Street. As Dorothy would say, 'It all just happened.' The Worker community consisted of whoever showed up at the door. The result was an assemblage of characters that seemed drawn from a novel by Dostoevsky.

Then came Mott Street, glorious, miserable Mott Street, with its opera-singing Italian neighbours and Mussolini statues in the shop windows. In April 1936 Dorothy and her co-workers moved into 115 Mott Street – five storeys of rat-ridden rooms in a rear building. With fresh paint, linoleum and curtains the place began to improve More than sixty people lived in Mott Street. Breadlines formed every morning and grew for a block and a half. By 1937 the house was serving 150 loaves of bread and seventy-five gallons of coffee every day. The line was two, three hours every morning.

There were now worker houses in Milwaukee, Detroit and Boston. Houses larger than the New York were springing up, with no prompting from Dorothy, in Pittsburgh and Chicago. Dorothy's speaking engagements began to bring in more money. She enlisted Steve and Mary Johnson, a couple who had arrived at the Worker, to look after Tamar. They provided Tamar with good meals and a lovely bedroom in their sunny apartment in the front section of the Mott Street building. Dorothy also made sure that Tamar visited Forster regularly. At Christmas and family gatherings they met with Forster, and Tamar played with her cousins.

A farm in Easton, Pennsylvania was the first property the Catholic Worker Movement owned. They bought it from a Polish family for $1,400 when they moved into Mott Street in April 1936. Through donations they had enough to buy it outright. Within a few months there were more than twenty people living on the farm – Jewish, Catholic, Greek Orthodox, Protestant and atheist.

In the following decades, Dorothy spent a good deal of time travelling around the country, visiting the houses of hospitality, speaking and reporting on the dramatic labour upheavals brought on by the Depression. From the sit-down strikes of the auto workers in Detroit, to the migrant workers in California, she made a point of going wherever there was trouble, wherever workers were resisting unfit conditions, to let them know that there were Catholics on their side.

## Poverty

From day to day, Dorothy and the whole Catholic Worker Movement did not know where the next money to pay the bills was coming from. They trusted in their co-operators and the readers of the *Catholic Worker* throughout the country.

Dorothy often spoke and wrote about living a radical poverty. She believed that we should rejoice in poverty because Christ was poor. In her thought and writings there are echoes of Pope Francis's call that the Church should go out 'to the peripheries'. Dorothy believed that in order to experience poverty we must love to live with the poor, because they are especially loved by Christ. It is not true love if we do not know the poor, and we can only know them by living with them.

In May 1952, Dorothy wrote:

> We live in a slum neighbourhood ... We need to be thinking and writing about poverty, for if we are not among its victims its reality fades from us ... We must talk about poverty, because people insulated by their own comfort lose sight of it ...

For Dorothy, precariousness is an essential element in true voluntary poverty. In May 1952 she remarked how, over and over again in the history of the Church, the saints emphasised poverty. She held that every religious community, begun in poverty and incredible hardship, but with a joyful acceptance by the rank-and-file priests, brothers, monks or nuns who gave their youth and energy to good works, soon began to 'thrive'. Property was extended until holdings and buildings accumulated; and although there is still individual poverty in the community, there is corporate wealth. It is hard to remain poor.

The experience of poverty could be more subtle for Dorothy, living, as she did in Mott Street. This poverty came from a lack of privacy, a lack of time to herself. Dorothy had cultivated tastes: she enjoyed the opera, well-prepared food and beautiful things. There was a fastidious side to her character, easily offended by noise and disorder. When the commotion in the woman's dormitory outside her room became too much to bear, she was known to open the door and shout 'Holy Silence!'

The spirituality of Dorothy Day was based on an effort to encounter Christ in our daily lives. Christ was present in the people around us, especially under the aspect of their needs, the needs of the most weak and vulnerable. To find Christ there, Dorothy held that we must become vulnerable too, for we cannot see our brother or sister in need without first stripping ourselves. Voluntary poverty was part of her spirituality.

# Prayer

In all her activities, Dorothy was strengthened by the daily discipline of prayer – daily Mass, the Rosary, at least two hours a day of meditation on Scripture. She liked to be alone in church for prayer. She would read and reflect upon the Psalms. She readily admits that often her prayers were 'half-conscious, and the planning, the considering, the figuring of "making ends meet" went on until she would catch herself out and turn to God again'.

Dorothy's daily speech and her writings were filled with references to Saints Paul, Augustine, Francis of Assisi, Teresa of Avila and her beloved Thérèse of Lisieux. They were her daily guides in the imitation of Christ. She relished the human details of their struggles to be faithful, realising that in their own time they were often regarded as eccentrics or dangerous troublemakers.

Dorothy's book, *Thérèse*, was published in 1960. What attracted her to Thérèse was certainly not *The Story of a Soul*, which Dorothy found colourless, monotonous, 'too small in fact for my notice', but rather Thérèse's blind faith, a naked faith in love. Thérèse emphasised that her way is a most ordinary way, a way open to all. Dorothy was also taken by the dark night of sense and soul that Thérèse was passing through, especially in the last months of her short life.

# War and pacifism

From its very beginnings the Catholic Worker Movement had adopted a pacifist stance, which position had not excited much reaction in the early years of the movement. This changed abruptly in 1936 with the outbreak of the Spanish Civil War. In the eyes of most Catholics, this was a Holy War, a crusade against atheistic Communism, and virtually every pulpit and Catholic newspaper in America supported General Franco. Dorothy's decision to take a neutral stance was a move that was guaranteed to provoke the outrage of many. It was Dorothy's conviction that Jesus Christ had come to offer a new definition of love as the ultimate law of our lives. The works of mercy could not be separated from the works of peace.

With the outbreak of the Second World War, Dorothy's pacifism faced its most terrible test. From the earliest days of Hitler's regime, Dorothy had picketed the German Embassy and warned in *The Catholic Worker* against the sin of anti-Semitism. In 1939, she helped to found the Committee of

Catholics to fight anti-Semitism, which challenged the anti-Semitism of the Catholic followers of Fr Charles Coughlin of Detroit, who preached an anti-Semitic stance on the radio in the 1930s. Coughlin also voiced some support for Hitler and Mussolini and made attacks on socialism and Communism.

After America entered the war against Japan and Germany, the Catholic Worker Movement continued with its pacifist stance. Dorothy declared that the manifesto of the movement was the Sermon on the Mount, which meant that they should try to be peacemakers. She often quoted the lines from Fr Zossima, a character in Fyodor Dostoevesky's *The Brothers Karamazov*: 'Love in practice is a harsh and dreadful thing compared to love in dreams.'

In September 1945, Dorothy was critical of President Truman's jubilant stance after the dropping of the atomic bombs on Hiroshima and Nagasaki. She quoted Truman's words: 'We have spent two billion dollars on the greatest scientific gamble in history and won.' Dorothy noted that America had killed 318,000 Japanese. She called it 'this colossal slaughter of the innocents'.

The Catholic Worker Movement wanted to act against war and the preparation for war: nerve gas, guided missiles, the stockpiling of nuclear bombs, conscription, the entire military state. Dorothy spoke of 'the hideous and cowardly war we are waging in Vietnam'.

The 500 pages of the FBI's files on the Catholic Worker Movement document the government's own exasperated efforts to classify the exact brand of subversion being perpetrated by Dorothy and her collaborators. The file discloses that the Director of the FBI, J. Edgar Hoover, for one, considered the movement dangerous enough to merit prosecution on the charge of sedition, and that he recommended such action to the Attorney General on three separate occasions. Hoover wrote:

Dorothy Day has been described as a very erratic and irresponsible person ... She has engaged in activities which strongly suggest that she is consciously or unconsciously being used by Communist groups.

This was the era of red hysteria in America – the fear of Communism infiltrating the country under any form.

## Cuba

By 1961, the Catholic Worker's sympathetic response to the Cuban Revolution had become a cause of perplexity and anger among many friends of the movement as well as among its critics. Were not the Communists in power avowed atheists? Had they not already expropriated extensive Church property and placed restrictions on religious education? How could the Catholic Worker reconcile its pacifism with a movement that attained its aim through violence? Dorothy's attempt, over the next year, to answer these questions served to intensify the controversy.

Fidel Castro held that he was not persecuting Christ but churchmen who had betrayed Christ. Castro had asked the clergy and religious to remain and teach when he took over the schools and nationalised Church property. Their reply was that priests and nuns would not teach Communism to their students. Castro, in turn, taunted them with the fact that all they thought of was money and property.

Dorothy wrote in July–August 1961:

> We are on the side of revolution. We believe that there must be new concepts of property ... We believe in farming communes and cooperatives and will be happy to see how they work out in Cuba ... God bless Castro and all those who are seeing Christ in the poor ...

One can imagine how those words went down with mainstream Americans at the time.

Dorothy embarked for Cuba on 5 September 1962. Her brief trip resulted in several long articles in the *Catholic Worker* in which she offered a generally positive account of the Cuban government's efforts in the areas of education, health, housing and employment.

In the 1960s, Dorothy hailed the Civil Rights Movement, but she remembered the decade as an angry and bitter time, which saw the assassinations of President Kennedy, Martin Luther King and Robert Kennedy. It was the era of anti-Vietnam protests and the students' revolution. Dorothy continued with her travels throughout the US, speaking on her great themes: the quest for freedom; community and peace; the sanctity of life; the dignity of the poor; the works of mercy.

## Travels abroad

In 1971, Dorothy visited India, where she met Mother Teresa of Calcutta, as well as the Gandhian centres of cottage industry. The same year, she made a peace pilgrimage to Russia and managed to 'disrupt' a meeting of writers by expressing her admiration for the writer Alexander Solzhenitsyn. From

Tanzania, she reported on President Julius Nyerere's experiments in village socialism. Wherever she went, she carried her diary, her breviary and a jar of instant coffee (she could not say which was the most essential!).

## Illness and death

A heart attack in 1976 put an end to Dorothy's incessant travelling and she accepted with gratitude this opportunity to decline the hundreds of invitations and requests to speak that continued to pour in. 'Tell them I'm in a state of nervous decline,' she would say to those in charge of making her excuses. She made no provision for the future of the Catholic Worker; she named no successor, established no formalised rule. The movement would endure if that were God's will. 'My job now is prayer,' she wrote. Still, she contributed something to the paper every month when she possibly could, even if only a few notes from her journal, 'to let people know I'm still alive'. Her last writing was about the beauty of nature, the loving-kindness of God, the need for more forgiveness, more mercy, more rejoicing.

Towards the end of her life, Dorothy's picture appeared in *Life* and *Newsweek*, accompanied by flattering profiles. She was cited by *Time* magazine in a cover story devoted to 'Living Saints'. Dorothy's reaction to this was to say: 'Too much praise makes you feel that you must be doing something terribly wrong.'

Dorothy died on 29 November 1980. She was eighty-three. Her body was buried on Staten Island in a plain pine coffin. Her funeral, attended by the hundreds of members of the Catholic Worker family, young and old, was, as she had prayed, an occasion for rejoicing. At the time of her death in 1980, Dorothy Day had already achieved iconic status as the 'radical conscience' of America.

In 2000, the Vatican officially recognised Dorothy's cause for canonisation. She is now called 'The Servant of God' Dorothy Day. Journalists have invariably cited her famous saying: 'Don't call me a saint. I don't want to be dismissed that easily.'

## The work continues

In a statement of aims and purposes frequently reprinted in the *Catholic Worker* the goal of the movement is simply: 'to realise in the individual and society the expressed and implied teachings of Christ'. Dorothy understood the Incarnation to be an ongoing fact. God had once and for all assumed our humanity, and we could not hope to know God without turning to our neighbours in love. Such love was not merely a passing glow, but something concrete and active. It meant extending fellowship, sharing bread with the hungry, clothing the naked, standing beside those who were outcast and persecuted.

Dorothy's spirit still lives on in the Catholic Worker – both the newspaper and the network of more than fifty communities across the US, which continue to hold out a vision of a 'society where it is easier to be good'. Countless thousands have been sheltered in the houses of hospitality, millions of meals have been served. Dorothy attached little importance to such figures. Hospitality, she insisted, meant more than serving a meal, offering a bed or opening a door; it meant opening one's heart to the needs of others. Like a true prophet, Dorothy combined denunciation of the world's injustice with annunciation of a new world – of forgiveness, solidarity and compassion – and she bore witness to that world in her daily living.

## Reflection

Sometimes when I am writing I am seized with fright at my presumption. I am afraid too of not telling the truth or of distorting the truth … Much as we want to, we do not really know ourselves … We do not want to be given that clear vision which discloses to us our most secret faults. In the Psalms there is that prayer 'Deliver me from my secret sins.' We do not really know how much pride and self-love we have until someone whom we respect or love suddenly turns against us.

# CHAPTER SEVEN

# Oscar Romero
## (1917–1980)

## Childhood

Oscar Arnulfo Romero y Galdámez was born on 15 August 1917 in Ciudad Barrios in the San Miguel region of El Salvador. This town in eastern El Salvador is not far from the border with Honduras. His father, Santos Romero, was the local telegraph operator and also ran a small farm. His mother was Gaudalupe de Jésus Galdámez. Oscar had five brothers and two sisters, one of whom died in infancy.

At the age of four, Oscar was stricken with polio. For a long time the disease affected his ability to move and to speak. From an early age he was an avid reader and was intrigued by words and their meanings. After three years at a local public school, Oscar was privately tutored by a teacher, Anita Iglesias, until he reached his teens.

## Seminary years

At thirteen, Oscar entered the minor seminary in San Miguel. It was run in a paternal and humane spirit by the Claretian Fathers and Oscar liked it there. After graduation he enrolled in the national seminary in San Salvador. In 1937, he was told that he was to study in Rome. A few days before he left for Rome, his father died.

While in Rome, Romero lived at the Pontifical Latin American College (*Pio Latino*) and studied at the Gregorian University, both of which were run by the Jesuits. He received his licentiate in theology in 1941. He remained in Rome, beginning doctoral studies in spirituality. He had a special veneration for Pope Pius XI, whom he called 'the Pontiff of imperial stature' for daring to confront totalitarian ideologies and regimes – Benito Mussolini and Adolf Hitler. Romero said of himself, somewhat prophetically: 'I learned from the imperial Pius XI the boldness to confront those in power fearlessly.'

## Return to El Salvador

Romero was ordained priest in Rome on 4 April 1942. Before finishing his doctoral studies he was summoned home by his bishop and he left Rome in August 1943. As a passenger arriving in Cuba from Italy (a country allied with Germany), Romero was suspected of espionage and was imprisoned in a concentration camp. He was set free when he was recognised as a cleric by a Cuban priest who had studied with him in Rome. He arrived back in El Salvador via Mexico in December 1943.

In the spring of 1944, Romero was appointed parish priest of Anamorós, a small, out-of-the-way village. After only two months there, however, the bishop of San Miguel called him back to be his secretary. Romero was also to assume responsibility for the city parish of Santo Domingo in San Miguel, whose church was temporarily being used as a cathedral. He was also put in charge of the secretariat of the diocesan offices. This workload would later put a strain on his health.

The Oscar Romero of the city of San Miguel (where he worked for twenty years) was known to be an accessible, generous man, charitable toward the poor. He regularly visited the prisons, helped sex workers to get off the streets and started an Alcoholics Anonymous group. During his time in San Miguel, he was accused of 'communism' because he had criticised how the *cafetaleros* (coffee-growers) exploited their workers.

In 1962, on the national holiday in El Salvador, a day that was supposed to celebrate the Fatherland, Romero commented:

> Which Fatherland? The one that rulers serve, not to improve but to enrich themselves? The Fatherland of wealth distributed in the worst possible way, in which a brutal social inequality makes the vast majority of those born on their own soil feel like rejects and foreigners? ... If someday the laws of the state trample down the divine law, then the Church will condemn those laws and forbid Catholics to abide by them.

In 1964, the government accused Romero of interfering in political matters and threatened to haul him into court. Romero was not intimidated. He defended his right as a priest 'to guide the people's consciences'.

1962 saw the opening of the Second Vatican Council. Romero published the Council's documents, commented on them and extolled them in the diocesan newspaper *Orientación*, of which he was editor. He continually quoted from the Council documents in his talks and writings. For Romero, the return to the Gospel was the characteristic, insistent note of the Council. His compass and guide was Pope Paul VI (1963–78), whom he praised as 'The Pope of dialogue ... leader of peace in the world ... the pilgrim of friendship among peoples ... the prophet of the development of peoples and social justice ... the genuine advocate of the poor against abuse by the rich.'

For some time Romero had been seeing a psychologist in order to relieve the nervous tension resulting from overwork and fatigue. The psychologist summarised his character as being 'an obsessive-compulsive perfectionist'.

In 1967, Romero was appointed rector of the inter-diocesan seminary of San José de la Montána in San Salvador. The seminary also housed the offices of the Episcopal Conference of the Archdiocese of San Salvador. Because of his efficiency, the Episcopal Secretariat of Central America and Panama also requested his services as secretary.

## Appointed bishop

In 1970, Romero was appointed an auxiliary bishop for the Archdiocese of San Salvador. He was fifty-three years old. During a retreat a few weeks later, he reflected in his spiritual diary on the circumstances of his nomination and his first reactions:

> Uncertain conscience, mixture of ambition, fear of not being qualified and having to resign, a sense of penance and reparation. My God, what uncertainty! I feel that I accepted almost without having fully reflected. I am trying, however, to make my decision conscientiously and correctly.

There is something attractive here about his sheer honesty and humanity. We may have had similar experiences in our own lives when we took on something while being unsure of our motivation and qualifications for the task.

Archbishop Luis Chávez of San Salvador did not force Romero to work in the diocese. In the seminary where he taught and lived as rector, Romero led a reserved, quiet, academic life. He had no close friends among the priests of San Salvador except for a Jesuit, Fr Rutilio Grande, who acted as master of ceremonies at Romero's ordination as auxiliary bishop.

## Liberation theology

These were the years of liberation theology. For Romero, the term *liberación* had to be understood correctly as *salvación*, otherwise he believed that one ran the risk of preaching merely political, immanent, materialist liberation and Marxist practices. Romero liked to speak of 'integral salvation', as did Pope Paul VI – the integral salvation of the human being as a whole, body and soul, with an earthly destiny and a heavenly destiny.

According to Romero, the one who expressed liberation theology in a wise, balanced way was Eduardo Pironio. This Argentine bishop stood out, for Romero, from the rest of the Latin American bishops because of his erudition, meekness and spirituality. Pironio was a friend of Paul VI who made him a cardinal in 1976. Romero had in his own personal library six books by Pironio, heavily marked and used. Romero publicly called him 'brother' and 'a great modern bishop'. He wholeheartedly agreed with what Pironio said in 1971:

> The Christian demand for justice is an integral part of the authentic preaching of the Gospel of peace. The religious message of the Church resides precisely in the total liberation of the person, which must not be identified with violence.

Politically, Romero was guided by the most basic principle: the common good of the country.

Meanwhile, the 1972 elections in El Salvador were marred by fraud, imprisonment, torture and exile. Romero observed that 'a tremendous sense of discouragement and fear, not to mention terror, is spreading in these days ... knowing, as we do, what sort of methods the current 'justice' system employs [the military and oligarchy]'.

## Bishop of Santiago de María

In October 1974, Romero was appointed Bishop of Santiago de María. The diocese had almost a half a million faithful and about twenty parishes. There were only about twenty priests, some of them elderly.

Some parishes had up to 50,000 parishioners and some had no priest. Romero had a jeep equipped with loudspeakers. Very often he could be seen setting out for the countryside early in the morning when people were going to work. He preached from the jeep in the open air, stopped to talk with people, administered the sacraments and distributed aid. He liked to be close to the poor.

Romero knew that some landowners, sometimes the ones who supported the Church, broke the laws about the minimum wage for rural workers. He began to voice requests for justice with regard to economic treatment:

> It saddens and concerns us to see the selfishness with which methods and arrangements are found to limit the just wage of the coffee harvesters ... 'Behold, the wages of the labourers who mowed your fields, which you kept back by fraud, cry out; and the cries of the harvesters have reached the ears of the Lord of hosts.' (James 5:4)

Romero denounced the injustices, beatings and outrages suffered by the Salvadorean *campesinos* at the hands of the landowners. The *campesinos* were not pariahs but 'citizens', besides being the children of God. They had the right to form unions. He called for the redistribution of land to favour a system of cooperatives. He wrote, 'A bishop intent on doing his pastoral duty can no longer speak without being branded a Communist.'

In the years 1970–74, Romero had emphasised the need for patient dialogue in social and political conflicts, the urgent need for structural reform based on conversion of hearts, the prophetic mission assigned to the Church, and the role of the priest, who should remain detached from politics while not neglecting the public forum.

In January 1976, Romero described his ideal of a bishop:

> A bishop can communicate the things of God and interpret history and human problems only in terms of the depth of faith. To be a sociologist, economist, or political scientist is neither his competence nor his task. He is simply a man of God in the service of his brothers and sisters ... A bishop is essentially a pastor, a father, a brother, and a friend. He journeys with other people, sows hope along their path, shares their sorrow and joy, urges them to seek peace, in justice and love, and teaches them to be brothers and sisters ...

Echoes of John XXIII's first homily as Patriach of Venice can be heard (see page 42).

# Archbishop of San Salvador

On 3 February 1977, Romero was nominated as Archbishop of San Salvador and thus the Catholic primate of the country. He had little time to prepare. He officially assumed the new role on 22 February.

At this time in El Salvador there was a military government, a highly privileged elite, many poor people, an emerging guerrilla movement and circles that dreamed about a Castro-style revolution. It was often said that fourteen families of the oligarchy controlled the entire Salvadorean economy. Since 1932 El Salvador had been governed uninterruptedly by the military, to which the oligarchy had delegated the task of keeping order in the country while they dedicated themselves to business.

In both 1972 and 1977 the presidential election results had been manipulated. The rise of guerrilla groups and popular organisations siding with the opposition was countered by repressive paramilitary units and then by death squads. The most feared private militia was ORDEN (Organización Democratica Nacionalista). It supported the landowners' interests in the countryside. One slogan of the extreme right was plastered on walls all over the country: *'Haga patria, mate un cura'* ('Be a patriot, kill a priest'). Priests were described as 'elements dangerous to national security'. Many Catholics in the popular organisations and in the guerrilla groups absorbed Marxist teaching and vocabulary.

The presidential election of 1977 was held on 20 February, just two days before Romero took office. Carlos Humbert Romero (no relation) won the presidency through fraud. The supporters of his opponents took to the streets to protest and a state of siege was proclaimed. The repression of public protests began during the night of 27 February. A massacre occurred. It was in this atmosphere of repression and terror that Oscar Romero began his ministry as archbishop.

Upon taking possession of the archdiocese, Romero had declined the offer of a large, comfortable house in one of the affluent neighbourhoods of San Salvador. He lived at the Divine Providence Hospital for poor, terminally ill patients. His residence consisted of a modest apartment that had been designed for a watchman. It had three small rooms with basic furniture and no hint of luxury. He said himself, 'I live in a hospital and experience suffering very close at hand, the groans of pain during the night, the sadness of those who are admitted.'

# Rutilio Grande

Romero first met his close friend Rutilio Grande when the Jesuit was president of the national seminary, which was subsequently closed down by the Salvadorean bishops. Romero and Grande became close friends despite the latter's commitment to a liberation theology that was far too radical for much of the Salvadorian Church. However, both men shared a hunger for a more just society.

On Sunday, 13 March 1977, just eighteen days after Romero's installation as archbishop, Rutilio Grande was murdered with two friends from the parish of Aguilares where he had lived since 1972. On his way to say evening Mass at El Paisnel, a little village close to Aguilares, Grande was gunned down in the sugar-cane fields along with Nelson, a fifteen-year-old boy and Manuel, an elderly *campesino*. All three died immediately, but the impact of those deaths had a tremendous significance on the future course of the Salvadorean Church.

Romero was shattered by Grande's murder. He stated later:

> When I looked at Rutilio lying there dead I thought if they have killed him for doing what he did, then I too have to walk the same path.

Romero confronted the outgoing President Molina, the government and the oligarchy head on. He urged the government to investigate, but they ignored his request.

On 15 March, the priests of the city of San Salvador met and asked that all priests concelebrate the funeral Mass in the cathedral the following Sunday morning, and that there should be only one Mass on that Sunday in the archdiocese, as a sign of unity. Romero, sceptical at first, decided to accept this unusual request. The Papal Nuncio, Archbishop Emmanuel Gerada, was opposed to this initiative and asked Romero to change this decision. Romero refused, writing to Gerada: 'It seems to me that an archdiocesan matter is within the exclusive purview of the archbishop.' This damaged relations with the Papal Nuncio who, a few weeks earlier, had worked to have Romero named archbishop.

The *missa unica* (the only Mass) took place on 20 March. Over 100,000 people poured into the plaza in front of the cathedral for the funeral Mass of a priest, an old man and a young boy. From the pulpit, Romero underlined that the Church's message was inspired by love and rejected hatred. The Mass was broadcast over the Church radio station. Speaking directly to their murderers, Romero said:

> We want to tell you that we love you and that we ask of God repentance for your hearts, because the Church is not able to hate, it has no enemies. Its only enemies are those who want to declare themselves so. But the Church loves them and dies like Christ: 'Father, forgive them, they know not what they do.'

Romero was to pay a high price for ordering that there would be only one Mass in the archdiocese that Sunday. He said later:

> This decision cost me a lot, but it was something that had a strong impact on the diocese, and it helped me feel courageous.

On 26 March, Romero travelled to Rome to receive his *pallium* – the insignia of his office as metropolitan archbishop – from Pope Paul VI. Afterwards, he met privately with Pope Paul, who said to him: 'Take courage, you are in charge!' He also met with Fr Pedro Arrupe, the Superior-General of the Jesuits, who assured him that the Jesuits in El Salvador were at his disposal. Romero felt heartened by these assurances. Complaints about Romero had not yet reached Rome. They would come later!

Emmanuel Gerada would become very critical of all of Romero's pastoral work, including his style of preaching. He even went so far as to suspect Romero of being connected with the guerrillas, though he believed that personally Romero was a man of religious and moral integrity.

## Tensions and violence

When he was appointed archbishop, no one could have envisaged that Romero would become a prophetic figure for Christians throughout Latin America. He was regarded as a safe compromise candidate in a Church that was dominated by a highly conservative hierarchy on the one hand and, on the other, by sections of the clergy who were highly committed to liberation theology. In fact, the divisions within the clergy very closely mirrored the deep divisions within Salvadorean society. The bishop of San Miguel, for instance, Colonel José Eduardo Álvarez, was Chaplain-General of the armed forces and regularly blessed helicopters before they embarked on counter-insurgency missions in the countryside which often destroyed entire villages. Meanwhile, many priests spent a great deal of their time documenting and protesting about large-scale human rights abuses committed by the army. The military were relieved at Romero's appointment as archbishop because they felt that he would take radical action to ensure that priests did not become involved in political activities. Many progressive Church people greeted the news of his appointment with extreme disappointment.

A political and populist myth about Romero speaks of his changing from being an arch-conservative to his becoming the moral leader of the Salvadorean people in the fight against the military dictatorship and the oligarchy. However, while Rutilio Grande's murder was a decisive element in moving Romero to take responsibility for the poor and for the people who were hostage to violence, it did not bring about a conversion in him. It would be more accurate to say that Romero did not have a 'conversion', strictly speaking, but an 'evolution', as he himself said in a radio interview. Fr Ricardo Urioste, Romero's vicar-general, said of him:

> Monseñor Romeo was a man who always kept changing when the voice of God was calling him to do something ... He discerned it in prayer, in conversation with God. He kept looking for what God was asking of him. He reacted as the Gospel called him to ... He certainly adopted an attitude of *fortalezza* (fortitude, courage) in the crisis surrounding him. He wanted to be a 'good shepherd', which was his life's ideal.

On 11 May 1977, another of Romero's priests, Alfonso Navarro, was killed. The previous day the body of Mauricio Borgonovo Pohl had been found. He had been Minister for External Affairs and belonged to one of the most powerful families of the oligarchy. He was kidnapped and murdered by a guerrilla group, the Popular Revolutionary Front (FPL). The FPL had demanded the release of thirty-seven prisoners in exchange for his safe return. The government stood firm and Pohl was executed. A far-right terrorist group chose to avenge his death symbolically by killing a priest. They erroneously thought Navarro was a Jesuit. In the morning Romero celebrated the funeral Mass for Pohl, whom he had known as a peaceful man, open to dialogue, and the funeral Mass for Navarro later on the same day. What interior struggle Romero must have suffered!

On 17 May 1977, a large contingent of government troops moved toward Aguilares, where four Jesuits from Rutilio Grande's group were still working. Up to 2,000 troops surrounded the town and besieged the church. They entered the church, opened the tabernacle, scattered the consecrated hosts on the floor and trampled on them. Romero rushed to Aguilares but was prevented from entering the town. The four Jesuits were arrested, beaten, driven to the Guatemalan border and expelled from the country. When the siege was over, some 400 citizens, men, women and children, lay dead. The massacre at Aguilares was an attempt to strike at the heart of one of the main popular organisations, the Popular Revolutionary Block (BPR) which was strong in the area. The BPR drew its support mainly from *campesinos*. It had taken over some land in the vicinity of Aguilares to grow crops, having exhausted all legal means to find work or permission to rent some poor and unused plots of land at a price the *campesinos* could afford.

As we have seen, the guerrilla opposition groups also used the tactics of kidnapping, murder, sabotage and damage to infrastructure. As the violence escalated, the Minister for Education, Dr Antonio Herrera, was killed, with his chauffeur, by one of the armed opposition groups. When journalists asked Romero about his solutions for El Salvador, he said: 'This is what I have always preached: the best, peaceful solution is a return to love and to a genuine desire for dialogue.'

Romero held in principle to the 'just war theory' of Thomas Aquinas, which stated that insurrection would be legitimate only if 'all peaceful means had been exhausted and if the evils of insurrection were not worse than the evils of the dictatorship or tyrannical power to be eliminated'. When Romero condemned revolutionary violence, he also denounced the injustices that provoked it. He said, 'We are in favour of non-violent opposition and a gradual transition to democracy, preferably without the spilling of blood.'

There were 229 priests in the archdiocese of San Salvador. Of these, 140 were religious, most of whom were not Salvadorean. There were about fifty Jesuits. The Jesuits ran the Central American University with its 3,500 students. In the countryside, the basic Christian communities were widespread. These communities came together to try to make sense of their work and living conditions in the light of the Gospel. Romero supported them. He took as his inspiration the encyclical letter of Pope Paul VI, *Evangelii Nuntiandi* (*On Proclaiming the Gospel*). This document emphasised the ecclesial (church) character of the basic communities and warned against drifting into politics. Nevertheless, Romero was accused of being indulgent with the popular organisation.

Romero's detractors, and he had many, even at the highest level in the Church in El Salvador, asked: 'How could a shepherd of the Church support a Marxist-Leninist?' This question was posed by his own bishops within the national hierarchy and underlined the bitter conflict that existed within the Church leadership at that time. Speaking of the division of the local hierarchy, Romero said that 'it just reflected the deep divisions which existed in Salvadorean society between the rich and the poor'. He spoke openly of his difficult situation:

> Some have treated me as a Communist; others today consider me as a traitor ... I run the risk that every preacher of the truth runs – that he will be misrepresented, that he will be slandered, that he will be persecuted ... The Church does not identify herself with any movement, any party, any organisation ... A bishop is not a politician. My perspective is pastoral and is based on the Gospel.

On one occasion the rival bishops produced two pastoral letters with two distinct themes. The division within the bishops' conference created such tensions within the Church that it nearly tore Romero apart internally, according to those who worked closely with him.

Romero had the support of Bishop Rivera Damas, the bishop of Santiago de María. Three other bishops – Álvarez in San Miguel, Aparicio in San Vicente and Barrera in Santa Ana – were hostile to him. He asked for a new auxiliary bishop, specifically Marco René Revelo. It reveals a certain naivety on the part of Romero. Revelo soon proved to be Romero's enemy. He sent negative reports about him to Rome and suggested that an apostolic visit to San Salvador be conducted by Bishop Antonio Quarracino in 1979 with a view to Romero's possible removal. (Bishop Quarracino would later become Cardinal Archbishop of Buenos Aires and predecessor to Jorge Bergoglio – Pope Francis)

Revelo's hostility towards him disappointed Romero so much that he eventually limited his auxiliary's duties to a single parish and dismissed him in November 1978. He listed the reasons for his decision in a letter to Cardinal Baggio, the Cardinal Prefect of the Congregation of Bishops in Rome: 'I never felt any support from him, any service ... never any fraternal communication.'

## Tensions but also support in Rome

On an earlier trip to Rome, 17–30 June 1978, Romero had met with Cardinal Baggio. Baggio did not conceal from Romero the fact that the Salvadorean bishops, except for Rivera Damas, had asked for his removal.

Baggio also criticised an honorary degree that the Jesuits at Georgetown University had conferred on Romero, saying that it was an obvious 'political trap'. Baggio told Romero, 'It does you no honour.' Lastly, the question of Romero's removal was addressed. Romero tells us, 'I put it in writing: if it is for the good of the Church, with great pleasure I will hand over to someone else this difficult government of the Archdiocese.'

On 21 June 1978, Romero met with Paul VI, whom he found to be cordial and generous. Pope Paul said to Romero: 'I understand your difficult task. It is a work that can be misunderstood and requires much patience, strength and hope … If there is anything I can personally do, I would be happy to do so … .' Romero also visited his favourite theologian, Cardinal Eduardo Pironio, and the Superior-General of the Jesuits, Fr Pedro Arrupe. Romero later wrote: 'Despite returning to my country, I am homesick for Rome … The Pope who is the true father of all, is there. I felt close to him.' Sadly, Pope Paul died later that year, on 6 August.

1978 was the year of the three popes. Karol Wojtyla was elected as John Paul II on 16 October. It took seven difficult months for Romero to establish a relationship with him.

On 14 December 1978, Bishop Antonio Quarracino of Argentina, suddenly showed up in San Salvador, without Romero being informed in advance. He was sent as a visitor to the archdiocese by Cardinal Baggio. Ironically, Quarracino's recommendations were the replacement of the Apostolic Nuncio, Emmanuel Gerada, who he thought unfit for the task. He also suggested retiring the bishops opposed to Romero and replacing them with a new generation of younger bishops. The Vatican hesitated to implement Quarracino's recommendations.

In May 1979, Bishops Alvarez, Aparacio, Barrera and Revelo sent a letter to the Vatican in which they blamed Romero for the violence in the country. The letter said that Romero had designed the pastoral approach of the archdiocese to incite class struggle, political extremism, revolution and the seizure of power by Communism. Romero's methods had brought an 'alarming crisis of faith in El Salvador among priests, nuns and lay people'. These four bishops tended to have good relations with the state and the oligarchy. They explained the violent acts against the Church as a tragic consequence of Marxist infiltration of the Church itself.

Romero noted bitterly several times the 'personal aversion' of these bishops towards him. Jealousies, rivalries, antagonisms and quarrels over jurisdiction were at the basis of these interpersonal difficulties. One of the accusations made against Romero was 'the priests now take their inspiration from the archdiocese of San Salvador rather than from their bishops'. Romero was reproached for being vain. The bishops argued that he was unorthodox, insane, severely ill psychologically and that he had been brain-washed by his advisers, especially the Jesuits.

## Civil war in El Salvador

By the autumn of 1979 El Salvador was in a deep economic and political crisis. General Romero's government showed itself to be totally incapable of coming to grips with the ever- expanding popular organisations and the increasingly effective armed opposition groups. There was a military coup on 15 October 1979 And General Romero left for the US. In a homily on 28 October, Archbishop Romero reminded the military that the constitution required them to guarantee the people's rights. The period of bloody repression continued, however, and El Salvador gradually slipped into civil war.

## The Sunday homilies

Throughout this period Romero's Sunday Mass from the cathedral had become a major focal point of resistance in the country. To ensure that his homilies reached the widest audience, they were broadcast on the Catholic Church's radio station, YSAX. During one of Romero's Sunday broadcasts, which could last as long as two hours, it was possible to walk down the street without missing a single word, because a transistor radio was on in nearly every home. Listening to the Romero's homilies was now regarded as a subversive act. During the homilies, he read out loud the latest list of those killed or 'disappeared'. Every week, with characteristic courage, he denounced injustices, reminding everyone that the poor were the real people and deserved the same protection under the laws as anyone else in El Salvador. He pleaded, 'If only the men whose hands are stained with murder listened to me!' The phrase 'only love liberates' was often on his lips.

In preaching, Romero felt that he was fulfilling his role as a bishop. The cathedral was the primary place of his activity. At the pulpit, he seemed to be transformed. He gained self-assurance and preached with power and authority. When he finished speaking, however, he was exhausted. Although the homilies were given at eight in the morning to avoid the tropical heat of the day, they seemed like fireside chats with close friends. He took few political or diplomatic precautions. Many described his homilies with one word – *verdad* (truth). He was unyielding in his defence of the victims of tyranny and in his affirmation of the rights of the poor. An expression that often occurs in Romero's homilies summarises their foundation: *Primeros Dios* (God first). God first established the natural law, which we must not violate by sin, oppression and violence.

In the last year of his life, Romero worked closely with a young priest, Raphael Urrutia. Urrutia said of Romero:

> He was a man unlike any other. He was shy, simple, intelligent, nervous, even irascible, but then he was ready to ask forgiveness for his temper. For him everything was urgent, everything had to be done immediately. But, above all, he was a man of prayer.

By this stage, Romero was constantly in the spotlight, in the press and on television. He was regularly being interviewed by foreign journalists about the situation in El Salvador. *Time* magazine (24 July 1979), depicted him as 'the most outspoken bishop in Latin America' in terms of human rights. The title of the article was 'An Archbishop without Fear'.

After the Sunday liturgy in the cathedral, Romero usually held a press conference. He maintained that this too was 'work to spread the kingdom of God on earth'. One of Romero's expressions, in particular, is universally known: 'If they kill me, I will rise again in the people of El Salvador.' A Guatemalan journalist, José Calderón Salazar, working for the Mexican newspaper *Excelsior*, claims to have heard Romero utter these words during a telephone conversation.

## Rome – meeting with Pope John Paul II

In late January 1980, Romero took advantage of being in Europe again. He had travelled to Belgium to receive an honorary doctorate from the University of Louvain, and he went on to Rome and to the Vatican. Pope John Paul II received Romero 'very warmly'. He gave him 'a strong embrace, told me that he was with me, and gave me a special blessing for my people'. Romero returned from Rome in a state of euphoria, strengthened by the full solidarity of the Pope, which had been expressed in personal, fraternal terms.

## Back home

El Salvador was slipping further into civil war. In the months of January and February 1980 almost 600 people were killed in the political violence.

Military repression caused most of the deaths. Romero preached, 'Violence is a regression of civilisation; it is the expression of man's primitive character.' He was tormented by what was happening. On 16 March 1980, he preached, 'We are incapable of reconciliation; we hate to the death. This is not the environment that God wants ... We need to learn to recite the Our Father and to say "Forgive us, as we forgive".'

## Fear of assassination

Romero knew that he could be killed at any moment. During his annual retreat in February 1980, he explained to his director, Fr Azcue:

> It is hard for me to accept the idea of a violent death, which in these circumstances is very possible ... I will cope with unknown circumstances with God's grace. He assisted the martyrs, and, if it is necessary, I will feel that he is very close as I offer him my last breath. But what matters more than the moment of death is to give him my whole life and live for him.

To Fr Azcue, Romero appeared 'terrified, like Jesus in the Garden of Olives'. Romero's agitation did not show when he was preaching or conducting official business, but, in his private life, he altered between serenity and depression. He experienced mood swings and sudden attacks of anxiety.

Although convinced that he was in serious danger, Romero chose not to hire protection, so as not to involve anyone else in a possible attack on his person. He travelled about alone in his car. In March 1980, he told the US ambassador, 'I only hope that when they kill me, they do not kill many of us ... Pastorally, it would be a negative witness if I travelled about in safety while my people were living in danger.'

On Sunday, 23 March, Romero preached in the cathedral:

> I would like to make a special plea to the men in the army ... before a man's order to kill, God's law, which says, 'Do not kill,' must prevail. No soldier is obliged to obey an order that goes against God's law ... The Church, defender of the rights of God, of the law of God, of the dignity of the human person, cannot remain silent in the face of the abominations ... In the name of God, then, and in the name of this suffering nation, whose increasingly tumultuous cries rise to heaven, I beg you, I plead with you, I command you, in the name of God – Stop the repression!

The next day, Monday, 24 March 1980, Romero was celebrating Mass at 17.30 in the hospital chapel for the repose of the soul of Sara de Pinto, an acquaintance of his. His last words at the end of the homily were: 'Let us unite together intimately then in faith and hope during this moment of prayer for Doña Sarita and for ourselves.' Just when he began the offertory of the Mass, a gunshot came from the entrance to the church. One shot from a marksman pierced Romero's temple and he died almost instantly.

## The funeral

On Palm Sunday, 30 March, Romero's coffin was mounted on the steps of the cathedral facing the Plaza Barrios, the central plaza in San Salvador. To accommodate the thousands who had come to pay their last respects to the murdered archbishop the Mass had to be celebrated outdoors. By eleven o'clock, as the Mass began, more than 250,000 Salvadoreans filled the plaza, sweltering in the morning sun. Cardinal Ernesto Corripio of Mexico was the chief celebrant, together with bishops from Panama, Peru, the US, Ecuador, France, Brazil, Spain, England and Ireland.

About twenty minutes after the Mass had begun the sound of an explosion reverberated throughout the plaza. Shooting started and panic broke out. Romero's coffin was rushed into the cathedral and swiftly interred in a special tomb because it was feared the attacking security forces would attempt to steal the remains. An hour later, some fifty people lay dead and hundreds were injured.

## Investigation into the murder

The investigation into Archbishop Romero's murder dragged on for fourteen years. There was no intention that it would go to trial during the civil war, which lasted from 1980 to 1992. Some 80,000 people died out of a population of four million.

A Commission on the Truth for El Salvador, established by the United Nations, finally reported to the Secretary-General of the United Nations on 15 March 1993. The report declared that a Major Robert D'Aubuisson gave the order to assassinate the Archbishop. The actual gunman has never been identified. Certain US diplomats described D'Aubuisson as a 'psychopathic assassin'.

Romero's burial plaque quoted a love poem that began: 'The kindest, meekest, most righteous, most handsome, noblest, holiest man had been killed.' During his first visit to El Salvador in 1983, Pope John Paul II entered the cathedral in San Salvador and prayed at Romero's tomb, despite opposition from the government and from some within the Church who strongly opposed liberation theology. Afterwards, the Pope praised Romero as a 'zealous and venerated pastor who tried to stop violence'.

On another visit to El Salvador in 1993, Pope John Paul II said:

> Romero is ours ... He belongs to the poor and the afflicted because he loved them with a sincere heart. He belongs to the Church because every time the Christian community searches for inspiration to live out its faith, Romero stands tall in the cloud of witnesses reminding us that it is possible – in fact, essential – to feel, to think with the Church (*Sentire cum Ecclesia*), as Romero's episcopal motto read.

## Romero – the martyr

On 3 February 2015, Pope Francis authorised Cardinal Angelo Amato, Prefect of the Congregation for the Causes of Saints, to promulgate Romero's decree of martyrdom. This cleared the way for him to set a date for Romero's beatification.

The beatification of Oscar Romero was held in San Salvador on 23 May 2015 in the Plaza Salvador del Mundo. Cardinal Amato presided over the ceremony on behalf of Pope Francis. An estimated 250,000 people attended the service.

Archbishop Romero was canonised on 14 October 2018 in St Peter's Square in Rome, along with Pope St Paul VI, his friend and supporter in dark days.

## Reflection

Lord, don't give me riches, don't give me a long or a short life, don't give me powers on earth that make human beings drunk with power, don't give me the madness of idolatry of the false idols of this world. Cleanse me, Lord, cleanse my intentions and give me the true wisdom of discernment, to distinguish between good and evil, give me the conviction that St Peter had of feeling myself loved.

CHAPTER EIGHT

# Pedro Arrupe
(1907–1991)

## Childhood

Pedro Arrupe y Gondra was born in Bilbao in north-western Spain on 14
November 1907. His father, Marcelino Arrupe, was an architect and his
mother, Dolores Gondra, was a homemaker. Pedro was the youngest in a
family of four sisters – Catalina, Maria, Margarita and Isabel. In 1914,
Pedro began studies at the school of the Piarist Fathers in Bilbao. In
August 1916, his mother died. Pedro was only eight years old. After the
funeral his father, Marcelino, took him to a local church and pointed to
the statue of the Virgin of Begoña and said to Pedro, 'From now on, she
will be your mother.' Pedro later recorded that he then understood 'more
than anything that God's mother was also my mother'.

## Medical student

After matriculating in Bilbao in 1923, Pedro applied to study medicine at
the Faculty of San Carlos at the Central University of Madrid. He was an
able student. In his first year, he won the first prize in anatomical studies.
In the second year, he won the prize for physiology and, in 1926, the prize
for therapeutics. While attending the university, Pedro also joined the St
Vincent de Paul Society, which exposed him to life in the poor suburbs of
Madrid.

## Lourdes

In 1926, when Pedro was nineteen, he was suddenly summoned to return
to Bilbao because his father was dying. After his father's death, Pedro and
his sisters, in the hope of taking their mind off their grief, made a pilgrimage

to Lourdes. Pedro went to the Medical Verification Bureau to offer his services as a medical student in the examination of cases and to verify any so-called 'miracle cures'. When speaking later of his experience of miracles in Lourdes, Pedro asked us to remember that he came from the School of Medicine in Madrid where he had so many professors (some truly renowned) and so many companions who had no faith and always ridiculed miracles. He had often heard his professors, who were atheists, speak of the 'superstitions of Lourdes'. Yet he was determined that he had been the eyewitness of a true miracle worked by Jesus Christ in the Eucharist.

During a procession of the Blessed Sacrament, a nun with Pott's disease (tuberculosis of the spine) lay on a stretcher. She looked up at the white host as it was carried past her in the monstrance. Suddenly, the nun rose from her stretcher and shouted 'I'm cured!' Arrupe was able to examine the nun and the X-ray photographs of her condition. He later described the event:

> In one solemn moment the paralysed nun and Jesus Christ came face to face. I don't know how they looked at each other. But in that instant there was a great contact of love between them.

A few days later, Arrupe was present to witness another miracle cure – this time of a seventy-five-year-old woman with advanced cancer of the stomach. After attending a procession of the Blessed Sacrament and praying fervently, she was walking around Lourdes in perfect health. Arrupe was there when the verifying doctors, many of whom were unbelievers or agnostics, X-rayed the woman's stomach. There was no trace of the cancer that had been plainly visible before.

Arrupe returned to Madrid to continue his medical studies. He felt unsettled, reflective, as if a decision was slowly maturing. He later said of his experience in Lourdes:

> There was born my vocation, in that atmosphere of both simplicity and grandeur at the feet of the Virgin Mary, midst the noisy insistent prayer of the pilgrims and the sweet murmurings of the river Gave.

## Joining the Jesuits

Early in January 1927, Arrupe announced to his sisters his decision to join the Society of Jesus. They were dumbfounded, as were his medical colleagues and professors. He entered the Jesuits on 15 January 1927 at the novitiate of Loyola in Guipúzcoa, in the Basque region of Spain. His fellow novices remembered him as a person of natural charm and great courtesy, with an excellent sense of humour and a beautiful baritone singing voice. He also had a great ability to mimic many different accents.

Early in 1929, Arrupe felt the first spark of a vocation to become a missionary in Japan. He wrote to the Jesuit Superior-General of the time, Wlodimir Lédochowski, stating his wish. He was disappointed in the reply which stated that he would be considered in the future.

The early 1930s saw Arrupe studying philosophy at the Jesuit College at Oña, situated between Burgos and Vitoria. It was while he was here that he had an intense mystical experience of an interior light through which he saw everything from a new perspective. He does not go into any detail about the content of the actual experience. On another occasion, he heard an interior voice say, 'You will be first.' Only much later did he realise the significance of this message.

## Jesuits expelled from Spain

In the general elections held on 12 April 1931, the Socialists were victorious. King Alfonso XIII decided to abdicate and leave Spain. On 14 April, a Socialist Republic was proclaimed under Niceto Alcalà-Zamora. In June 1931, a new, blatantly anti-clerical constitution was promulgated. The newspaper *El Sol* of 14 October had the headline: 'Society of Jesus to be dissolved and all its assets nationalised.' The Jesuits were given a few days to leave the country. The Jesuit students of Oña, Burgos, were transferred to Marneffe, Belgium. Arrupe continued his philosophical studies at St Francis Xavier College in Marneffe between 1932 and 1933.

## Ordination and mission to Japan

From 1933 to 1936 Arrupe pursued theological studies at Ignatiuskolleg, Valkenburg, Limburg, in the Netherlands. In July 1936, he did his pre-ordination retreat at Marneffe with the famous Jesuit scholar, Fr Pedro de Leturia, as the retreat director. Arrupe was ordained priest in Marneffe, along with thirty-nine other young Jesuits on 30 July 1936.

On 15 September 1936, Arrupe left the port of Antwerp, Belgium, bound for New York. He completed a fourth year of theology at St Mary's College, Kansas (1936–37). He then proceeded to do his Jesuit tertianship (a third spiritual year before taking final vows) at St Stanislaus Novitiate,

Cleveland, Ohio (1937–38). On 6 July 1938, he received his assignment for the Japan mission from the Superior-General, Fr Lédochowski, some nine years after his original petition.

On 30 September 1938, Arrupe sailed from Seattle for Japan, arriving at the Port of Yokohama, Tokyo, on 15 October. For the first year he pursued Japanese language and culture studies at Nagatsuka, Hiroshima. He then became assistant parish priest of Yamaguchi. Ever since his days as a novice he had dreamed of being a missionary in Japan, like the great apostle of the East, St Francis Xavier. Here he was now in the very parish where the great saint began his work in Japan.

## Imprisonment

On 8 December 1941, the military police of Yamaguchi, the Kempetai, searched Arrupe's house. He was brought to the military prison under suspicion of espionage. He was accused of preaching *heiwa* (peace) to his parishioners. To talk of peace in time of war was considered to be an act of sabotage.

Arrupe was placed in solitary confinement for thirty-four days. He was shoved into a cell of four square metres. He was enveloped in darkness. He wrote of this time:

> I passed the days and nights in the cold of December entirely alone and without a bed or table, or anything else but a mat on which to sleep. I was tormented by my uncertainty of why I was being imprisoned ... But I was above all tortured by not being able to say Mass, at not being able to receive the Eucharist. What loneliness there was! I then appreciated what the Eucharist means to a priest, to a Jesuit, for whom the Mass and the tabernacle are the centre of his life.

Arrupe tells us that he learned wisdom and inner dialogue 'with the guest of my soul' during his long hours of solitary confinement. Years later in Rome, he confessed that this was the 'most instructive period of my life':

> It was beautiful – the solitude with Christ ... I learned the knowledge of silence, of loneliness, of harsh and severe poverty, the interior conversation with the guest of my soul who had never shown himself to be more 'sweet' than then.

On 12 January 1942, thirty-seven hours of continued interrogation began. Then, on 17 January, he was suddenly released.

## Master of Novices

Arrupe returned to Yamaguchi and was quickly assigned to be Vice-Rector of the novitiate house San Juan de Goto, and Master of Novices in Nagatsuka, Hiroshima. Arrupe's novices remember him as an extraordinary teacher, filled with good humour. He frequently slept for only four hours on a plank without a mosquito net. He would sometimes be seen cleaning the shoes of the novices. He would start the day with an hour in the chapel, sitting Zen fashion, immobile, on his heels.

Years later, Arrupe confessed:

> My novices were sufferers, yet at the same time impenetrable. It was necessary to dismantle their conception of God in order to take them to a greater God. Before the War, the Emperor was God. When they discovered a greater God, they experienced astonishment.

The Japanese novices had also to be disabused of their pride and egoism and bombast. They had to learn humility. Arrupe would make them go into Hiroshima and walk behind horses, collecting the horse dung with a spade and bucket!

## The atomic bomb

During July–August 1945 arguments raged as to whether or not the atomic bomb should be used against Japan. The Japanese no longer had enough food in stock and their fuel reserves were strained to the limit. Emperor Hirohito was in favour of peace initiatives, but it was the military that were the power behind the Japanese throne. The Japanese tended to idealise death at the expense of life. From a Japanese soldier total sacrifice was demanded.

On 1 June 1945, after much soul-searching, the committee advising US President Truman unanimously recommended that an atomic bomb should be released on Japan as soon as possible.

On 6 August 1945, an American B-29 bomber, the *Enola Gay*, appeared in the sky over Hiroshima, a city with a population of some 245,000. The atomic bomb, with a force of 17,000 tons of TNT, destroyed around 60,000 of Hiroshima's 90,000 buildings. Up to 100,000 people died instantly. Within four days, the total dead reached some 150,000. Arrupe and the novices helped to raise some pyramids of bodies and pour fuel over them to set them alight.

The Jesuit novitiate building was some distance from the city and, though damaged, the building was still habitable. The Jesuit community took in around 150 victims of the bombing. Arrupe used his desk as an operating table. He performed the surgical operations without any anaesthetic. They had neither chloroform nor ether nor morphine. The community tore up shirts and sheets to make bandages. What struck Arrupe was that the patients all suffered in silence. He found their self-control and stoicism remarkable.

On 9 August another atomic bomb was dropped on Nagasaki, a city of around 200,000. More than 70,000 would die without trace. Some hours later, Emperor Hirohito delivered the news of the defeat and surrender of Japan. Arrupe would say later that it was not the atomic bomb that was the final cause of the end of the war, but the order of the emperor.

Of the 150 or so victims that the Jesuits took into the novitiate, only two died. Six months later, having been cared for, all left the house. Some among them had been baptised. Arrupe comments on this: 'All had learned that Christian charity knows how to understand, help and give a consolation that surpassed all human comforting.'

## Post-war years

On 11 February 1950, Arrupe wrote to his nephew, informing him that he was translating four books into Japanese – the life of St John of the Cross; the life of St Francis Xavier; *Dialogue with Marxism*; and *The Truth about Communism*. In 1954, Arrupe was appointed Vice-Provincial of Japan. He was to be superior of some 200 Jesuits in Japan, comprising twenty-nine nationalities.

In November 1954, Arrupe began to travel in Europe, Latin America and the US. During these journeys he spoke of his Hiroshima experience. His objective was also to find help for Japan. He indicated how the apocalypse of Hiroshima had changed his life, how it had deepened his sense of dependence on God.

In 1958, Japan became an autonomous Province of the Society of Jesus and Arrupe was chosen as its first provincial. By now, he had also established himself as a wide-ranging thinker and prolific writer. He was the author of eight books in Japanese, including the aforementioned life of Francis Xavier; a commentary on the Spiritual Exercises of St Ignatius and a translation of the works of St John of the Cross.

## Superior-General of the Society of Jesus

On 22 May 1965, Pedro Arrupe was elected the twenty-eighth Superior-General of the Society of Jesus at its thirty-first General Congregation in Rome. In August 1965, he made his annual eight-day retreat. In his personal retreat notes, he writes:

> All the gifts and graces have been granted not for myself but for the Society and the Church...My attitude before the Lord has to be one of the deepest humility and gratitude. The post for which he has chosen me requires an extraordinary purity of soul ... here you have me at your disposal, Lord ... He [the Lord] is the one who directs; I have nothing else to do but to listen. He inspires; I try to put this into practice ...

Arrupe refers in the same notes to the need for:

> ... 'internal solitude' and the need for prolonged prayer on one's own (preferably at night) and also brief, but intense prayer in difficult circumstances in which one asks from God the solution to a problem, these are the most propitious moments ... A deep and very clear feeling of the real presence of Jesus Christ in the Eucharist. Jesus Christ is really present in the tabernacle. He, the Saviour of the world, of all creation, the Head of the Church and of the Society. He is there and He speaks to me.

On 27 September 1965, Arrupe spoke at the Second Vatican Council about how the Church was failing to transmit its truth, its principles. He spoke on atheism and on the missionary activity of the Church. He offered input during the debate on the Vatican Council document on the Church in the Modern World (*Gaudium et Spes – Joy and Hope*). Arrupe spoke here on the crucial task of inculturation of the Gospel message.

In 1967, Arrupe was elected President of the Union of Superiors General of all male religious orders. He was re-elected to this post in 1970, 1973, 1976 and 1979. In April 1968, he travelled to Medellín, Colombia, along with Pope Paul VI. While in Latin America, he sent a letter to all the Jesuits there:

> We cannot remain silent, in certain countries, before regimes which constitute, without any doubt, a sort of institutionalised violence.

Arrupe participated in the Synods of Bishops in Rome in 1969, 1971, 1974, 1977 and 1980. The Synod of 1971 produced the document *Justice in the World*, which would have a further influence on Arrupe's thought and his leadership of the Society of Jesus.

In July 1973, Arrupe gave a memorable address in Valencia, Spain, to the International Congress of Jesuit Alumni. His theme was that of the Bishops' Synod of 1971, the Synod on Justice. Arrupe stated that the prime educational objective of the Society of Jesus must be to form men and women for others – men and women who cannot conceive of love of God that does not include love for the least of their neighbours; men and women completely convinced that love of God that does not issue in justice for others is a farce. Arrupe asked the rhetorical question, 'Have we Jesuits educated you for justice?' He responded to his own question, 'No, we have not!' He continued by telling his audience:

> To be drugged by the comforts of privilege is to become contributors to injustice as silent beneficiaries of the fruits of injustice … We cannot separate personal conversion from structural reform … Egoists dehumanize themselves … Egoism and injustice are built into the very structures of society.

In the same speech, Arrupe expressed the need for greater simplicity of life, for attachment to fewer belongings, for a society in favour of the weaker. The address did not go down well with the audience, most of whom came from bourgeois families and enjoyed wealth and high social standing. The press came out against Arrupe – his address had been full of 'impertinence'. However, Cardinal Villot, the Vatican Secretary of State, wrote to Arrupe to thank him for his evangelical message.

On 26 January 1975, Arrupe was interviewed on RAI, Italian national television. The interviewer asked him, 'Who is Jesus Christ for you?' Arrupe said afterwards that the question took him by surprise and that he answered it in a completely spontaneous way:

For me, Jesus Christ is everything. He fills my whole life. He appears in the features of Jesus Christ in the Eucharist. Jesus Christ is the motor of my life. Take away Jesus Christ and everything will fall down ... The heart of Christ as a symbol of love has sustained me greatly in my life and has given me the key to understand the Lord without difficulty. Jesus Christ is a friend to me, especially in the Eucharist.

Writing to his sister Maria for her golden jubilee in the Sacred Heart Order, Arrupe mentions his little private chapel, like a cathedral, his source of atomic energy:

A mini-cathedral! Just eighteen feet by twelve ... this little oratory was the fountain of incalculable power and dynamism for the whole Society, a place of inspiration, consolation and strength ... Where the Master's glance and mine cross each other, where one learns much in silence ... This cathedral is the theatre of the most important act of the entire daily routine: the Mass ...

On 9 February 1979, at a press conference in Puebla, Mexico, the usual attacks on the Jesuits were forthcoming – they were accused of being socialists and communists and were being blamed for the troubles in El Salvador. Arrupe replied:

The Jesuits in El Salvador are working for justice and are doing a good job. When in July they were threatened that if they didn't leave the country they would be killed, I told them to stay. The Order will not be moved by threats ...

# Resignation?

After sixteen years as Superior-General, Arrupe considered resigning. This was not as simple as it sounds. No previous Superior-General of the Jesuits had ever resigned and Arrupe had to ask the permission of Pope John Paul II. He was granted an audience on 18 April, 1981. The audience lasted thirteen minutes as the Pope was just about to depart for Paris. On 1 May 1981, the Pope wrote to Arrupe asking him not to resign. On 13 May 1981, the Pope was shot in St Peter's Square by Mehmet Ali Agca. Arrupe went to Gemelli Hospital to see him.

On 6 August 1981, the thirty-sixth anniversary of Hiroshima, Arrupe gave an impromptu address to the Jesuits working with refugees in Thailand. It turned out to be his last public address. Of particular note are two short paragraphs:

I will tell you something I ask myself very often: Should we give spiritual help to the guerrillas in Latin America? No, you say? Well, I cannot say no. Perhaps in the past I have. But they are human beings, souls who are suffering. If you have a wounded person, even if he is a guerrilla, you have to help him. That is the meaning of the Good Samaritan. Is this political? People say so. But no, I am a priest now. I am helping this poor person. I don't care if he is a guerrilla, a religious, or a non-Catholic. He is a poor person. He is a person who is suffering.

I will say one more thing, and please don't forget it. Pray. Pray much. Problems such as these are not solved by human efforts. I am telling you things that I want to emphasise, a message – perhaps by 'swan song' – for the Society. I am so happy, and I think it is providential that I came here.

## A major stroke

On 7 August 1981, Arrupe suffered a major stroke at Fiumicino Airport while returning from the Philippines via Bangkok. Pope John Paul II sent a message of sympathy. On 31 December 1981, the Pope mentioned that he would like to visit Arrupe in the infirmary of the Jesuit headquarters near the Vatican. There is a photograph of this emotional meeting. Fr Arrupe, with some difficulty, said to the Pope: 'Holy Father, I renew my obedience and the obedience of the Society of Jesus to you.' The Pope is said to have replied: 'Father General, sustain me with your prayers and your suffering.'

Fr Arrupe was to live in the infirmary for almost ten years. It was to be a long *via crucis* – the way of the Cross. In July 1983, Fr Pedro Miguel Lamet SJ went to Rome to interview Arrupe personally for a biography he was writing. Lamet spent an hour or two with Arrupe every day for twenty days. He sometimes found Arrupe in a state of depression. He is reported to have said to Lamet:

I am so alone and no good for anything. Terrible, terrible. I was always so happy ... Only with God, alone, alone, everything broken, broken, futile … I must suffer it. It is life. God is above all this always … My life is to be with God. We must see God in everything. I don't understand this, but it must be from God, must be His providence. Something special for the Order and me. Now and again I feel a strength, a very special strength … The Lord gives me light. I want to give everything to the Lord. Everything is difficult. This is what God allows, something special he has sent us … It is tremendous, tremendous …

In his resignation speech on 3 September 1983 (written for him by those who knew his mind and heart best) Fr Arrupe said:

Now, more than ever I find myself in the hands of God. This is what I have wanted all my life since my youth. But there is a difference: the initiative is entirely with God. It is indeed a profound spiritual experience to know and feel oneself so totally in God's hands.

## Final illness and death

And so the years passed in the infirmary, Arrupe's purgatory on earth. He was totally dependent on others for everything – a man, once so active, reduced to helplessness. Finally, on Sunday, 27 January 1991, when his state of health showed clear signs of deterioration, the Superior-General, Fr Peter Hans Kolvenbach (elected in 1983), made a request for the Pope's blessing for Arrupe. That very evening Pope John Paul came himself to visit Arrupe and to impart his blessing. He stood at the bedside in silent prayer for some moments, then recited some prayers with the Jesuits present and gave his blessing to Fr Arrupe. Arrupe was unconscious and could not say goodbye.

After almost ten years of waiting, Fr Arrupe finally died on 5 February 1991. On the day of his death the Pope praised Arrupe for his 'profound piety, his zeal for the church, and his generous and patient acceptance of the divine will in his sufferings'.

The solemn funeral Mass took place in the Church of the Gesù, Rome, on 9 February. The funeral was attended by crowds that filled the piazza outside the church. Also in attendance were ten cardinals, twenty bishops, Italian Prime Minister Giulio Andreotti, as well as other religious and civil dignitaries. The chief celebrant at the funeral Mass was, according to ancient tradition, the Master-General of the Dominicans, Fr Damien Byrne OP. The homilist was the Jesuit Superior-General, Fr Peter Hans Kolvenbach. On either side of the altar were Pope John Paul's representative, Cardinal

Martinez Somalo, and the Jesuit cardinal, Carlo Maria Martini, Archbishop of Milan. Some 350 priests concelebrated the Eucharist. When the final blessing was finished, young Jesuits lifted the coffin onto their shoulders, and the hymn 'In paradisum' (Into paradise) was intoned. Immediately there exploded in the church a long, enthusiastic applause, which continued all along the streets.

Father Arrupe's body was initially buried in the Jesuit mausoleum in the cemetery of Campo Verano outside Rome. In June 1997, it was brought back from Campo Verano to be laid to rest in the Church of the Gesù. A sepulchre had been prepared alongside an altar in the right nave, marked with a medallion with Arrupe's effigy.

The Jesuit liberation theologian, Jon Sobrino, said of Fr Arrupe: 'Here lies a man so human: he had a heart larger than the world in which he lived. One cannot help but love him.'

Arrupe had great respect for Jesuit palaeontologist Pierre Teilhard de Chardin. He would often recite de Chardin's prayer: 'Lord, enclose me in the depth of your Heart. And when you have me there, burn me, purify me, set me afire, raise me up to the perfect satisfaction of your pleasure, unto the most complete annihilation of myself.' It would appear that the Lord had heard Arrupe's prayer.

On 11 July 2018, the Superior-General of the Jesuits, Fr Arturo Sosa, announced the beginning of the process for Fr Arrupe's beatification.

## Reflection

Nothing is more practical than finding God, that is falling in love in a quite absolute, final way. What you are in love with, what seizes your imagination, will affect everything. It will decide what will get you out of bed in the morning, what you will do with your evenings, how you spend your weekends, what you read, what you know, what breaks your heart, and what amazes you with joy and gratitude. Fall in love, stay in love, and it will decide everything.

# CHAPTER NINE

# Mother Teresa of Calcutta
(1910–1997)

## Childhood

Gonxha Agnes Bojaxhiu was born in Skopje, capital of Macedonia, on 26 August 1910. She was the third of three children, having a brother and sister. Her parents were devout Roman Catholics, especially her mother. In 1919, when Agnes was nine, her father died of apparent poisoning after attending a political meeting. He was a municipal counsellor with strong nationalist convictions. Nevertheless, Agnes tells us: 'We were all very united, especially after the death of my father. We lived for each other and we made every effort to make one another happy.'

At the age of twelve, Agnes felt her first calling to religious and missionary life. With the encouragement of her parish priests, who were Jesuits, her interest in missionary outreach grew. With the guidance and help of a Jesuit, Agnes eventually applied for admission to the Order of the Sisters of Our Lady of Loreto (commonly called 'The Irish Sisters'). Agnes was attracted by their missionary work in India.

## Ireland and India

At eighteen years of age, Agnes left her home in Skopje on 26 September 1928 to travel to Ireland to join the Loreto Sisters. She travelled by train through what was then Yugoslavia, Austria, Switzerland, France and England until she arrived at the mother house of the Sisters of Our Lady of Loreto in Rathfarnham in Dublin. She had two months of intensive English language studies and then set sail for India on 1 December 1928. After a five-week journey, she arrived in Calcutta on 6 January 1929.

Agnes and the other young sisters with her did their novitiate in Darjeeling in the foothills of the Himalayas. She made her first profession of vows on 25 May 1931, taking the name 'Teresa' after her patron saint, Thérèse of Lisieux. She tells us: 'I chose Teresa for my religious vows. But it wasn't the name of the great Teresa of Avila. I chose the name of the Little Flower.'

## The teacher

Teresa was assigned to teach geography and history at Loreto, Entally, one of the six schools run by the Loreto Sisters in Calcutta. She would remain in this profession until 1948, when she left the Loreto Sisters to establish the Missionaries of Charity. She summed up her life in these years: 'I was the happiest nun in Loreto. I dedicated myself to teaching. That job, carried out for the love of God, was a true apostolate. I liked it very much.'

In a letter to her former Jesuit confessor in Skopje in 1937, Teresa writes of just having received permission from the Mother General of the Loreto Sisters to pronounce her final vows. 'What a great grace!' she writes. But then her letter continues:

> Do not think that my spiritual life is strewn with roses – that is the flower which I hardly ever find on my way. Quite the contrary, I have more often as my companion darkness. And when the night becomes very dark – and it seems to me that it will end up in hell – then I simply offer myself to Jesus ... I need much grace, much of Christ's strength to persevere in trust, in that blind love which leads only to Jesus crucified. But I am happy ... I would not wish to give up my sufferings ... I am laughing more than I am suffering ... so that some have concluded that I am Jesus' spoiled bride who lives with Jesus in Nazareth – far away from Calvary ... I beg you, pray always for me.

This letter to her confessor back in Skopje is the first instance in her correspondence where Teresa refers to 'darkness'. It is difficult to grasp what 'darkness' meant for her at this time – spiritual desolation, spiritual dryness, an apparent absence of God from her life, and, at the same time, a painful longing for God? She was not enjoying the light and consolation of God's sensible presence but rather striving to live by sheer faith.

On 24 May 1937, Teresa pronounced her final vows as a Loreto sister. The ceremony took place in the convent chapel in Darjeeling with Archbishop Ferdinand Périer of Calcutta presiding. Following the Loreto custom, Teresa was now called 'Mother Teresa'.

Mother Teresa returned to Calcutta to continue her teaching. On Sundays, she used to visit the poor in the *bustees*, the slum areas of Calcutta. She chose this extra apostolate herself.

In April 1942, she made an exceptional private vow:

> I made a vow to God ... to give God anything that He may ask, not to refuse Him anything. I wanted to give God something very beautiful and without reserve.

This private vow was one of Mother Teresa's greatest secrets. No one except her confessor knew about it. When she finally referred to her special vow seventeen years later, she revealed its significance: 'This is what hides everything in me' (Retreat Notes, 1959).

In 1944, Mother Teresa was appointed principal of St Mary's High School for Bengali girls on Convent Road, Calcutta, as well as being in charge of three or four Loreto sisters and the de facto superior of the Daughters of St Anne (the Bengali congregation affiliated with Loreto). By 1946, due to pressure of work, Mother Teresa was weak and ill. A period of enforced rest culminated in the directive to go on retreat to the hill station of Darjeeling. The intention was that in the interests of her health Mother Teresa would undergo a period of spiritual renewal and a physical break from work.

## The train to Darjeeling – mystical experience

During the train journey to Darjeeling on Tuesday, 10 September 1946, Mother Teresa had a decisive mystical encounter with Christ:

> It was in that train I heard the call to give up all and follow Him into the slums ... to serve Him in the poorest of the poor ... I knew that it was His will and that I had to follow Him. There was no doubt that it was going to be His work.

Mother Teresa considered this day, celebrated later as 'Inspiration Day', to be the real beginning of the Missionaries of Charity. From that day onwards, she began to receive a series of interior locutions (voices) that continued until the middle of the following year. She was hearing the voice of Jesus and conversing intimately with him. She would usually refer to these communications as the 'Voice'. The 'Voice' kept pleading: 'Come, come, carry Me into the holes of the poor. Come be my Light.'

Mother Teresa related what had happened on the train to Darjeeling during her retreat to her spiritual director, Fr Celeste Van Exem SJ. His first request to her was to stop thinking about the inspiration, to let it rest. By January of 1947, Van Exem had no doubt that Teresa's inspiration was from God and so he gave her permission to speak to Archbishop Périer of Calcutta. In her first letter Teresa told the Archbishop of her inspiration and of how there were many holy souls longing to give themselves only to God. She wrote: 'European orders are too rich for them – They get more than they give.' She told the Archbishop that she heard the 'Voice' distinctly saying:

> I want Indian nuns, victims of My love, who would be Mary and Martha, who would be so united to Me as to radiate My love on souls. I want free nuns covered with My Poverty of the Cross.

Archbishop Périer remained cautious and told Teresa that he needed time to pray, reflect and consult.

Shortly after Teresa wrote her first letter to Archbishop Périer, her provincial had notified her of her imminent transfer from Calcutta to the Loreto community in Asanol, a town about 140 miles to the north-west. Some sisters of Teresa's Loreto had noticed that she was having frequent and long conversations in confession with Fr Van Exem in the months following her retreat in Darjeeling. From this simple fact, suspicion arose concerning the nature of their relationship and, therefore, the decision was taken to transfer Teresa to Asanol.

Meanwhile Archbishop Périer had expressed to Fr Van Exem his three concerns: first, he questioned how much Mother Teresa's self-will and self-interest were involved; second, he considered the reported request of Jesus to approve Mother Teresa's request to be a thanksgiving for Archbishop Périer being a bishop for twenty-five years as too sentimental; lastly, he wondered if the change to Asanol might have provoked her request to leave the Loreto order and start a new congregation.

## Persistence

Undaunted, Mother Teresa had heard that Archbishop Périer was going to Rome and so she wrote to him:

I would be grateful if you spoke to the Holy Father about the project. He will understand. It will depend on you, Your Grace, to tell the Holy Father everything ... Tell our Holy Father of my longing to be all things to all men.

Somewhat annoyed by Teresa's insistence, the Archbishop attempted anew to explain his measured course of action:

I am neither opposed nor in favour of your project and, as Archbishop, I cannot be anything but neutral at this stage ... The question is too important for the Church to decide all at once. It may take months, it may take years ...

Teresa responded:

While you are in Calcutta, could you not do the needful through the Apostolic Delegate and then when the little Institute is on its feet apply to Rome for recognition? ... Don't delay, Your Grace, don't put it off. Your Grace, forgive me for being so tiresome with my continual appeal, but I have to act in this way.

Archbishop Périer asked Teresa to set out her exact plans. She replied that Our Lord wanted Indian nuns, 'victims of His love'. They would work among the poorest of the poor. The first year of their religious life would be one of complete contemplation – and solitude – which would be renewed every six years, after they had taken vows. Girls from the age of sixteen upwards, strong in mind and body and with plenty of common sense, would be accepted. In their second year of training the sisters would attend maternity and other nursing training.

In July 1947, Mother Teresa returned to the Loreto community in Calcutta. This change took place at the intervention of her Superior-General, Mother Gertrude M. Kennedy, who believed that 'Mother Provincial was mistaken ... in her estimate of Mother M. Teresa.'

During 1946–47, Mother Teresa enjoyed an intense degree of union with Our Lord. Years later, she recalled this extraordinary time:

Before the work started there was so much union – love, faith, trust, prayer, sacrifice ... The sweetness and consolation of those six months passed but too soon.

120

Fr Van Exem continued to be Teresa's advocate with the Archbishop, stating that it all came from God. Teresa pleaded with the Archbishop in October 1947: 'I beg you, Your Grace, in the Name of Jesus and for the love of Jesus to let me go.' She wrote to the Archbishop an account of three visions she had had – of a great crowd of very poor people, calling out 'Come, come, save us – bring us to Jesus.' There was another great crowd with sadness on their faces. Teresa heard Our Lady telling her to take care of them. She had a vision of Our Lord on the Cross, of Mary at a little distance from the Cross and Teresa in front of it. The Crucified Jesus asked her: 'Will you refuse to do this for me – to take care of them, to bring them to me?'

Mother Teresa wrote to the Cardinal Prefect of the Sacred Congregation of Religious in Rome asking to obtain an 'indult' of secularisation, which would free her from the vows that bound her to the Loreto congregation. In that letter she wrote:

> The thought of leaving the Institute of the Blessed Virgin [Loreto] breaks my heart. Why Almighty God calls me now to this new life I do not know, but I want to do His Most Holy Will without any reserve, whatever the cost may be.

On 8 August 1948, Teresa was granted an indult of exclaustration authorising her to stay outside the Loreto convent and to keep her vows under the authority of Archbishop Périer.

## Mother Teresa leaves Loreto

On 17 August 1948, clad in a white sari with a blue border (symbolising her desire to imitate the Virgin Mary), Mother Teresa set out to begin life as a Missionary of Charity. She left with just five rupees. Her destination was the Holy Family Hospital of the Medical Sisters in Patna, where she was to learn the basics of nursing needed to serve the poor.

On 21 December 1948, Mother Teresa went into the slums for the first time as a Missionary of Charity. Soon the slum dwellers were calling her 'the Slum Sister'. She said, 'I am glad to be just that for His love and glory.' After two months of searching, the third floor of a home on 14 Creek Street was made available to become 'the first home of the Missionaries of Charity'. Mother Teresa tells us, 'After 1949, I saw young women arriving one after another. All of them past students of mine. They wanted to give everything to God and they were in a hurry to do so.'

In the first Rules of the Congregation, Mother Teresa identifies their special mission:

> The particular end is to carry Christ into the homes and streets of the slums, among the sick, the dying, the beggars and the little street children. The sick will be nursed as far as possible in their homes. The little children will have school in the slums. The beggars with be sought and visited in their holes outside the towns or on the streets ... Our particular mission is to labour at the salvation and sanctification of the poorest of the poor, not only in the slums, but all over the world wherever they may be. (*Constitutions* 5).

Mother Teresa grasped the depth of Jesus' identification with each sufferer and understood the mystical connection between the sufferings of Christ and the suffering of the poor. Through her humble service, she endeavoured 'to bring souls to God and God to souls'.

## The Society of the Missionaries of Charity

In March 1950, Mother Teresa wrote to Pope Pius XII asking for the approval of the new congregation as a diocesan institute. By June 1950, the community numbered twelve. With the permission of the Holy See, Archbishop Périer officially established the Society of the Missionaries of Charity in the archdiocese of Calcutta on 7 October 1950. On 11 April 1951, the first group of sisters began their novitiate as Missionaries of Charity.

The city of Calcutta provided Mother Teresa with one of the shelters at the Kali Temple. There the sisters would bring the dying off the streets and offer them accommodation, basic medical care, and, above all, tender love. Teresa regarded this shelter as the 'treasure house' of her congregation, which 'housed Christ in distressing disguise'.

By the end of 1952, the third floor of the house on Creek Street had become too small for the community of twenty-six members. After storming heaven with prayer, Teresa found a house on 54A Lower Circular Road. The Archbishop approved the purchase and advanced the necessary money and so the Missionaries of Charity moved into what remains their motherhouse to this day. The community moved there in early 1953.

# Mother Teresa's spiritual state

During the early years of the congregation, Teresa wrote to Fr Van Exem and to Archbishop Périer of 'a darkness and loneliness of soul'. In January 1955, Teresa wrote to the Archbishop about her 'deep loneliness'. She continued:

> There is such a deep loneliness in my heart that I cannot express it. For months I have not been able to speak to Fr. Van Exem ... Pray for me, for with me everything is icy cold. It is only blind faith that carries me though for in reality to me all is darkness ... There is that separation, that terrible emptiness, and feeling of absence of God.

To this baring of her soul, the Archbishop answered with a short summary of the teaching of St John of the Cross on the 'dark night'. Archbishop Périer pointed to the great success of the mission as a sign of the God's presence: 'God's blessing is in your work.'

During her yearly retreats, Mother Teresa would review her life and renew her commitment to strive after holiness. In April 1957, she made known to Archbishop Périer her determination to uproot the defects of her strong personality. She admitted that she had sometimes been rather quick and harsh in voice when correcting the Sisters. Another resolution was to become 'an apostle of joy – to console the Sacred Heart of Jesus through joy – I want to smile even at Jesus and so hide if possible the pain and darkness of my soul even from Him ... The smile is a big cloak which covers a multitude of pains.'

## Superior-General

In 1959, Teresa wrote to the Archbishop suggesting that because of his advanced age and delicate health, the congregation be allowed the independent governance envisioned in the Constitutions, while remaining under his guidance. The Archbishop agreed and appointed Mother Teresa to be Superior-General. He also approved her proposal to begin foundations outside of Calcutta. Two new missions were opened in Delhi and Ranchi late that year. There were now eighty-five sisters and fifteen more to come, with leprosaria in fifty-two centres in Calcutta.

# Travels and foundations abroad

Meanwhile, the accomplishments of Mother Teresa's community began to attract admiration and praise as articles describing her work began to appear locally and internationally. In July 1960, the Catholic Relief Services of New York, on behalf of the National Council of Women, invited Mother Teresa to their national convention in Las Vegas. On 25 October 1960, Teresa left India for the first time since disembarking in Calcutta in January 1929. In Las Vegas, over 3,000 women were waiting to hear the 'simple little unknown missionary'. Before her trip, Mother Teresa had written, 'Imagine me in U.S. in front of those thousands of great people. I would die of fear and shyness.' Once there, she spoke about 'her people' and the work in the slums and ended by inviting all to share in the 'works of love'.

From the US, Mother Teresa went to England, Germany, Switzerland and, finally, Italy. After her return to Calcutta on 1 December 1960, she confided to Archbishop Périer: 'My going to the U.S. was the hardest act of obedience I had ever had to give to God.'

In April 1961, Fr Joseph Neuner, a Jesuit who taught theology in Pune, India, was invited to preach a retreat to the Missionaries of Charity in Calcutta. Mother Teresa attended the retreat and spoke to him privately. Fr Neuner was able to impart to Mother Teresa invaluable insight into her spiritual trials, which she appreciated greatly: 'I have come to love the darkness ... For I believe now that it is a part, a very, very small part of Jesus' darkness and pain on earth.' She wrote to Fr Neuner: 'A hearty "Yes" to God and a big smile for all.'

On 28 April 1962, Mother Teresa was presented with the *Padri Sri* (Order of Lotus), an award given to Indian citizens for their outstanding work. The honours bestowed upon her and her work accentuated the absence of intimacy with Jesus that she longed for. She confided to Fr Neuner: 'I had to go to Manila for the Magsaysay Award. It is one big sacrifice. Why does He give all these but Himself? I want Him not His gifts or creatures.'

On 25 March 1963 the Missionaries of Charity Brothers, the first male branch of the Missionaries of Charity family was established. On 1 February 1965, the Missionaries of Charity received the hoped-for pontifical recognition whereby the congregation was placed under the authority of the pope instead of the diocesan bishop. Because the Inter-nuncio, Archbishop Robert Knox, was the official representative of the pope, he came from

Delhi and summarised the spirit of the congregation in three words – dependence, detachment and dedication. Mother Teresa shared with Archbishop Knox her joy at the opening of the first foundation outside India in Venezuela.

In the early 1970s, Pope Paul VI granted Mother Teresa Vatican citizenship to facilitate her missionary travels. In 1975, the Missionaries of Charity celebrated the silver jubilee of their foundation. They now numbered more than a thousand sisters in eighty-five foundations in fifteen countries.

It was during this time that Mother Teresa met Fr Michael van der Peet, a priest of the Sacred Heart, while on a visit to Rome. They corresponded afterwards. She told him how she made her Holy Hour with Jesus straight after Mass 'so I get two hours with Jesus before people and Sisters start using me – I let Him use me first.' Though she labelled her prayer 'miserable, dry and frozen', she felt that it proved effective and obtained graces for others.

Fr van der Peet rejoiced in the privilege of his exchange with Mother Teresa. 'It was a gift from God for which I am most grateful.' He later admitted: 'The impression that I got was that I was dealing with a woman who somehow saw God and felt God in the distress of the poor and a woman who had incredible faith in light and darkness. She saw the suffering of Christ, but it was not that she was taken up in ecstasy or things like that – that was not part of her life, although people might be tempted to think that ... I really believe that the reason Mother Teresa had to undergo so much darkness in her life is that it would bring about a greater identification with the poor.'

## A public figure

BBC journalist Malcolm Muggeridge came to Calcutta in the spring of 1969 to make a documentary on Mother Teresa and the work of the sisters. He had only five days in which to do the filming in the Home for the Dying. 'The home was overflowing with love,' Muggeridge said afterwards, 'and the love was luminous. God's invisible omnipresent love. A miracle.' He called the film *Something Beautiful for God*, wrote a book with the same title, and became an active campaigner on behalf of Mother Teresa's work. He was also among those who lobbied support for her nomination for the Nobel Peace Prize. Muggeridge's documentary made Mother Teresa famous in the West, not only in Catholic circles but in wider society. As a consequence, she was awarded the Good Samaritan Award in the US, the Templeton Award for Progress in Religion in England and the Pope John XXIII Peace Prize at the Vatican.

Being a public figure was a real suffering for Mother Teresa. Yet her smile, a 'cloak' that covered this pain, prevented others from sensing what living in the spotlight cost her. To smile required an effort, as she explained during a speech in 1977:

> I remember some time ago a very big group of professors came from the United States and they asked, 'Tell us something that will help us.' And I said, 'Smile at each other.' I must have said it in a serious way and so one of them asked me, 'Are you married?' And I said, 'Yes, and I sometimes find it very difficult to smile at Jesus because He can be very demanding.'

## Nobel Peace Prize

In November 1979, at the Fourth General Chapter of the Missionaries of Charity, Mother Teresa was again elected Superior-General. Shortly afterwards, on 11 December 1979, she received the Nobel Peace Prize. The usual celebratory banquet was cancelled at Mother Teresa's request. She said that she would rather the money was used for those who were really in need of a meal, and the £3,000 earmarked for it was duly added to the prize money of £90,000, together with a further £36,000 raised by young Norwegians. Asked why she had decided to come to receive the Nobel Prize in person, she made the point that would become the leitmotif of her public statements in Oslo. She was grateful for the gift that would provide housing for the homeless and for the leper families, but she was especially grateful for the 'gift of recognition of the poorest of the poor of the world'. 'I am myself unworthy of the prize. I do not want it personally. But by this award the Norwegian people have recognised the existence of the poor. It is on their behalf that I have come.'

She accepted the prize from King Olaf V of Norway. At the acceptance speech in the Aula Magna (Great Hall) of the University of Oslo, Mother Teresa did not deviate from her practice of speaking without notes. Before delivering a speech prepared only with the sign of the cross she called upon her audience to recite the Prayer of St Francis. As Fr Van Exem commented afterwards, 'Only Mother could have got away with it.' She said:

I feel that greatest destroyer of peace today is abortion, because it is a direct war, a direct killing, direct murder by the mother herself ... That unborn child has been carved in the palm of the hand of God ... I find the unborn child to be the poorest of the poor today ...

The message relating to the life of the unborn child in particular was potentially an unpopular one in a country that had recently made state-financed abortions readily available. Mother Teresa did not compromise her convictions for the occasion.

On Tuesday, 11 December, all the newspapers in Oslo carried pictures of Mother Teresa on their front pages. One Norwegian journalist wrote:

How good it is to experience the world press for once spellbound by a real star, with a real glitter, a star without a wig, without a painted face, without false eyelashes, without a mink and without diamonds, without theatrical gestures and airs. Her only thought is how to use the Nobel Prize in the best possible way for the world's poorest of the poor.

From the moment she became 'Mother Teresa, the Nobel Prize winner', the attentions of the press would rarely abandon 'the saint of the gutters'.

## Illness and death

While visiting the Congregation's community in Rome in 1983, Mother Teresa fell out of bed and was hospitalised. A serious heart condition was discovered. In spite of this she devoted much of her time and energy in the last years of her life to the development and growth of the male branches of her religious family. The Missionaries of Charity – Contemplative was made up of priests and brothers and was founded in 1979. The Missionaries of Charity Fathers began in New York in 1984.

Mother Teresa was re-elected Superior-General in 1985. Pope John Paul II visited the Home for the Dying in Calcutta on 3 February 1986. By the end of 1989, Teresa's heart condition was worsening and she was at death's door several times. Yet, in the 1990s, there were new foundations in Russia, Cuba, Ethiopia, Southern Yemen, Nicaragua, the Czech Republic, Hungary and Albania.

In 1994, Mother Teresa was in Vietnam to open a new house. In 1996, President Bill Clinton signed legislation making her an honorary US citizen. She remained at the head of her congregation until March 1997, when

Sister Nirmala Joshi was elected her successor. In June 1997, Mother Teresa received the Congressional Gold Medal of Honour.

On 5 September 1997, Mother Teresa suffered a heart attack and died at 9.30 pm. She was eighty-seven. She had been asked by so many to slow down and rest and she always said, 'I have eternity to rest.'

On 26 July 1999, the cause for the beatification of Mother Teresa was officially opened in Calcutta. Pope John Paul II had granted an exemption to the general regulation that such proceedings can be taken up only five years after the death of the subject. Teresa was beatified on 19 October 2003, and Pope Francis canonised her at a ceremony on 4 September 2016 in St Peter's Square.

## Reflection

O Jesus, you who suffer, grant that today and every day I may be able to see you in the person of your sick ones and that, by offering them my care, I may serve you. Grant that, even if you are hidden under the unattractive disguise of anger, of crime, or of madness, I may recognise you and say, 'Jesus, you who suffer, how good it is to serve you!' Give me, Lord, this vision of faith, and my work will never be monotonous. I will find joy in harbouring the small whims and desires of all the poor who suffer ... O God, since you are Jesus who suffers, be for me also a Jesus who is patient, indulgent with my faults, who looks on my intentions, which are to love you and to serve you in the person of everyone who suffers. Lord, increase my faith. Bless my efforts and my work, now and for ever. Amen.

# CHAPTER TEN

# Roger of Taizé

(1915–2005)

## Childhood

Roger Louis Schutz-Marsauche was born on 12 May 1915 in the small village of Provence, fifteen miles from Neutchâtel, Switzerland. His father, Karl Schutz, was a Protestant pastor, a man who had decided at an early age to study theology, and who had pursued his studies first in Berlin and then in Paris and Switzerland, where, for many years, he wrote commentaries on the New Testament. Years later, Roger would say of his father, 'My father was an intellectual which I am not, but ever since he was young he had a great love of the poor.'

Roger's mother, Amélie Marsauche, was more artistic. Her family, Huguenots from Burgundy, had been Protestant since the Reformation. Music had always played a prominent role in her life and she had studied singing in Paris.

Roger was his parents' ninth and last child. His only brother was considerably older and so it was his seven sisters who featured prominently in his early recollections. He played alone a good deal. Solitude in the garden left a deep impression on him – the beauty, the discovery of everything in the garden, a woodpecker, a whole host of things that had their roles to play in the life of the garden.

The Schutz home was always full of music. There were two and, at one stage, even three pianos in the house, and, at a very early age, Roger developed a special love for Bach and Chopin and music in general. His youngest sister, Geneviève, remembers him singing in his room with a very fine voice.

When Roger was five years old, he spent a Sunday with his sisters in the countryside. Towards the end of the afternoon, they entered a Catholic church. Roger remembered,

Everything was bathed in shadows except for the light that illumined the Virgin and the reserved sacrament. The image remains with me still.

One day, on a walk in the Swiss Alps, Roger's father, Karl, broke off from the party to enter a Catholic church alone. Roger remembered that his father remained there praying for a long time and eventually emerged without saying anything. Roger recalled:

This fact influenced me profoundly. If he went there to pray, it must be because he found there something about which he did not speak but which must be very powerful.

In the village of Provence where he lived Roger was struck by the fact that Christians went to pray on Sundays in two different places: some to a church, others to a hall. They passed each other on the street. When he was a child Roger used to talk very readily about how he would organise his life when he was an adult. Everything was to take place in a large country house where there would always be lots of people. He had planned a kind of 'harmony' for the day and there would always be a generous and expansive welcome.

## Struggle for faith and a time of illness

At thirteen, Roger began his secondary schooling in a town some distance away. He lived in the house of a Catholic widow, Madame Bioley. She was a woman of deep Catholic faith who took Communion every day. Roger said later:

It goes without saying that having lived with them, the Catholic faith at its most generous, its most essential, touched me greatly.

When Roger spoke of these years, he tended to see in them a period of a type of 'agnosticism' or of 'not-being-able-to-say-fully-I-believe', rather than radical disbelief. Lengthy conversations with Madame Bioley always revolved around the question of belief: 'How is belief possible?' Roger always remembered that Madame Bioley left an indelible mark on him: 'She was a living expression of the Gospel's sovereign freedom.'

It was Roger's confidence in the integrity and faith of his parents that was to help him through a period of what he insists was not complete agnosticism but rather an inability to pray, of silence in the presence of God. He wrote:

> I could not altogether doubt the existence of God. I have never been able to place the existence of God in doubt. What was in doubt was communion – communication. I could not in all honesty pray ... I put my trust in the faith of my parents and grandparents.

Roger later attributed his own striving for sensitivity of approach, his passion for listening to others, and his desire for an understanding of that 'great ocean of the heart' to the darker, even painful, interludes in his life. In his teens, he fell ill with tuberculosis. He was ill for several years, during which there were intervals of apparent improvement and relapse and even a time when he was close to death. His recovery was a slow and protracted process. He had to spend a period of enforced solitude during which he read, studied and eventually managed to take long walks in the mountain air. With hindsight, Roger recognised that he managed to traverse later difficulties in his life more serenely because he came close to death at an early age.

## University studies

Having recovered from his illness, Roger bowed to his father's wishes and, in 1936, applied to study theology for four years at the universities of Lausanne and Strasbourg. In the summer of 1937, his first year of study was over but his doubts about faith and his chosen course of studies returned. Was this really the way for him? Should he continue? What happened then was one of those events which often mark our future destiny. Lily, one of his married sisters, was due to give birth and was gravely ill. The outcome seemed certain to be fatal. Roger tells us, 'Then, perhaps for the first time ever, I really prayed. A very poor prayer! I simply said a psalm to God.' But it was a step forward. Lily lived. For Roger, it was like a miracle, an answer to his prayer.

At Strasbourg, while studying one day, Roger came across the lines, 'It is Christ who enables us to know God. Do not seek elsewhere.' He tells us later that these lines brought home to him that it was through Christ that those around him looked at, penetrated the invisible, perceived a reflection of the unseen.

During his final years of university studies, Roger was chosen against his wishes as President of the Christian Students' Association. It was, however, a step that brought him into contact with other young people. They were questioning themselves on religious faith. Meetings were held in the faculty of literature room at Lausanne.

Out of a group of regular attendants at these meetings a year later, under Roger's leadership, the 'Grande Communauté' was to be born. This was a group that would meet regularly for colloquia and for retreats, which Roger described as 'necessary for much converse with God and little with his creatures'.

During his long walks, Roger used to go into a little isolated parish church where he would meditate upon the idea of community. He experienced what he referred to as 'a kind of instinct … a certainty that something was going to happen'. Roger used to stay at Valsainte, the only extant Carthusian monastery in Switzerland. He found himself captivated by the life of prayer, and by the fact that the monks prayed and lived in community. So great was his interest that his father was afraid that Roger would never leave!

## Second World War

By now the Second World War had begun and France had been defeated by the Nazis. Nevertheless, Roger began to think about how he might live in France:

> I found myself as if impelled to do everything I could to build a community life in which reconciliation would be realised, made concrete, day by day. To begin with, I must start a life of prayer alone. I would find a house where there would be prayer in the morning, at midday and in the evening and I would take in those who were fleeing, those in hiding.

At Lausanne, Roger assembled his closest student friends. He tells us,

> I invited those from the science and arts faculties, but no theologians because I told myself theologians would want to chat about God!

Almost without exception, his student friends did not want to go to France – understandably!

## Cluny and Taizé

Notwithstanding their reluctance, Roger himself set off alone for Burgundy on a bicycle. After several days, he arrived in Macon and, having read the history of the nearby monastery of Cluny, determined to visit the site. He heard that there was a house for sale in nearby Taizé. It was a poor area. The house had stood empty for several years. A neighbour showed him around. Then, since time was moving on, Roger asked the neighbour, an old woman, where he could find something to eat. The old woman replied that he had best come and eat with her since there was no shop or café nearby. During the simple meal, Roger told the lady something of his ideas and, all of a sudden, he heard her saying,

> Stay here, we are so alone. There is no one left in the village and the winters are so long and cold.

The words of a poor, ageing woman were to prove decisive. Roger could not know that at the same moment the actual owners of the house for sale, living destitute in Lyon, had decided to offer a novena that their house might find a buyer. The owner of the house, Madame de Brie, a woman of considerable piety, went to Mass for the ninth day of the novena and returned home to hear that Roger Schutz would buy her house!

## La Communauté de Cluny

When Roger returned to see his parents in Geneva and recounted to them what he had done, his father said, 'God speaks through the poorest of the poor. You must listen to the humility of that humble woman.' In Lausanne, Roger gathered some thirty friends to reflect on his dream. Out of that group was to evolve the first 'community' – not the brothers, but a network of friends who met regularly every two months, lived with a common rule of life and were associated with Roger through the early years under the name *la communauté de Cluny*. During 1941, Roger had written an eighteen-page pamphlet in which he outlined his monastic ideal for a life of communion. It was the Beatitudes that spoke to him most:

> I have always considered the Beatitudes to be essential texts and I began with the three words that encapsulated the spirit of the Beatitudes – joy, simplicity and mercy. In them was the essential of the Gospel.

## The first brothers

Among those who read the initial pamphlet were two students who were later to become the first brothers of Taizé. Max Thurien was studying theology in

Geneva and Pierre Souvairan was reading agriculture in Zurich. They came to join Roger in a flat in Geneva. They were joined by a fourth, Daniel de Montmollin, and together they embarked on a life of common prayer and work, committing themselves provisionally to celibacy and community of material possessions with a promise that would be renewed annually.

Max Thurien was preparing a dissertation on liturgy and Roger eventually defended his doctoral thesis on 30 April 1943. The subject of the thesis was 'The ideal of monastic life before Saint Benedict and its conformity to the Gospels'. That theme, and the study of many early monastic rules that it entailed, was clearly not chosen by chance. In 1943, Roger was also ordained a Lutheran pastor.

## Living in Taizé

'Reconciliation' was the ideal of Taizé from the very beginning, reconciliation in the common life, 'That they may all be one … ' (John 17:21). With the liberation of France in the autumn of 1944, Roger and three prospective brothers moved to the house at Taizé. The first years in Taizé after the war were harsh. German prisoners of war were housed near Taizé and the brothers would visit them, sharing their food and prayer with them. Roger believed that where compassion is lost, everything is lost. The local population had never been understanding and the welcome the brothers offered to German prisoners didn't make their life any easier.

By 1947, thanks to the agricultural skills of one of the brothers, the community was producing enough to become relatively financially stable. It also provided a welcome for a steady flow of visitors, among them not only Catholic priests and religious but also Protestant theologians, for whom common prayer of a twentieth-century monastic community was of special interest. At Pentecost 1948, the village church was made available for the brothers' common prayer by a *simultaneum*, a system in parts of France by which authorities may agree to the additional use of a Catholic church building for Protestant services. The authorisation was signed by Angelo Giuseppe Roncalli, then Papal Nuncio in Paris, but subsequently to become Pope John XXIII, 'that man so large of heart', who was to place such immense trust in Taizé.

Robert, the first French brother, joined the community while he completed his medical studies. Robert later became the local doctor at Taizé. Two others followed him – Axel and Albert. With them we have the complete list of the seven brothers who, in the little Romanesque village church, took the three traditional monastic vows at Easter 1949, committing themselves for life to celibacy, to community of goods and the acceptance of an authority represented by the figure of the prior.

## The Vatican and ecumenism

In 1948, the Vatican's Holy Office published a text that effectively forbade Catholic participation in ecumenical meetings. Roger went to Rome and met a certain Monsignor Giovanni Baptista Montini at the Vatican. (Monsignor Montini would subsequently become Pope Paul VI in 1963). Roger described their meeting: 'It was utterly wonderful because Monsignor Montini understood everything and it was from that time that a spiritual friendship began.' Roger, no doubt through the influence of Monsignor Montini, managed to meet Pope Pius XII. Roger begged Pope Pius:

> Leave a little way open, even a narrow one and define what you consider to be the essential barriers – but leave a way forward. Do not close it altogether.

The following year, the Holy Office issued another text granting local bishops the responsibility of deciding whether Catholics within a diocese should take part in ecumenical activities.

## A parable of communion

From the very beginning, Roger wanted the community to be a real parable of communion, a parable of reconciliation, open to a future that embraced the concrete and visible unity of all Christians. He wrote himself:

> We are here because of Christ and the gospel, and Christ has, in a sense, called us to recapture the image of a reconciled Church. That is the point of the vocation of the Taizé community. There is this wounded Christ whom we wish to follow in the unique communion that is his body, whom we do not wish to abandon. We wish to be a small reflection of what that communion is for everyone, a small reflection of the Church that is constantly reconciling itself.

Roger contemplated the example of Jesus during his trial – Jesus, calumniated, said nothing in reply. This was an example that Roger learned to emulate: 'All my life when people have taken me to task I have struggled to remain silent.' He had also learnt not simply to react but to nourish the importance of what he called 'spiritual tack'. There can be little doubt, however, that, at times, the breakdown of communication between members of different denominations caused Roger great personal suffering. The question as to what had been among his greatest trials wrested from him a fleeting sigh of sadness, not recrimination – 'the failure of churchmen to understand the essential of what we are trying to live'. There were times in the beginning when he found communication easier with those who were not churchmen, and times also when his intentions were misrepresented or disfigured.

## 'Fraternities' of Taizé

By 1951, as soon as there were twelve brothers, two went to live and work in the mining area thirty miles from Taizé. They were called the first 'fraternity'; the Rule was soon to state that the brothers, wherever they went, were called to be 'signs of the presence of Christ among people, and bearers of joy'. From that moment, Taizé was always partly 'abroad', with small groups of brothers forming 'fraternities of Taizé' in various parts of Europe, then later across the world – the slums of the Mathare Valley in Kenya; Puerto Rico; Japan; South Korea; Calcutta; Bangladesh.

## Rome and Taizé

During the winter months of 1952/53, Roger withdrew into silence and in his retreat wrote out the Rule of Taizé. In the years 1952, 1954 and 1955, representatives from Taizé were invited to meetings in Rome, but Roger referred to those years, without criticism, as a period in which there was a certain 'emptiness'. In 1958, Pope Pius XII died, having privately expressed regret that he had not concerned himself sufficiently with ecumenism.

Three days after the inauguration of Pope John XXIII, Roger and Max Thurien were summoned to a papal audience. Roger recalled,

> He was so interested and when we spoke of reconciliation he clapped his hands and exclaimed 'Bravo'. He was such a simple man, so open, so full of joy and spontaneity ... That audience gave a new stimulus to our ecumenical endeavours. From then onwards, Pope John had an unexpected

influence on us, and, without knowing it, let a little springtime be born in Taizé.

A meeting of a similar kind was to take place annually with Pope John. The Church of Rome had assumed a more open and welcoming face.

In September 1960 and 1961, Roger invited a dozen Catholic bishops and approximately fifty Protestant pastors to meet at Taizé for three days. The gathering that ensued was the first of its kind to take place since the Reformation and, in order that those present should not dwell on the divisions of the past, Roger invited them rather to share with one another the common pastoral concerns each was experiencing in the contemporary world. In particular, he drew attention to the situation in Latin America, a situation about which, at the time, Europe was showing little concern.

## The Church of Reconciliation

By the late 1950s the little church in Taizé could no longer contain the people who were beginning to flock to the Sunday services. There could be no question of turning away the growing number of young people, but Roger admitted that their advent was something for which he had not been prepared:

> What I had envisaged was a small group, a few men bound for life by a commitment to a life in God, a life of prayer, a contemplative life, but who would work and would not look for anything else. We could never have imagined what was to follow.

To his first brothers, Roger had one day confided that they would confine the community to twelve, yet that early vision had already eroded.

A German delegation that had been founded after the war by German Christians to construct signs of reconciliation in places of wartime suffering sent representatives to Taizé. This organisation offered to raise funds and provide volunteer work to construct a new church as a sign of reconciliation.

The Church of Reconciliation was built during 1961–62 by a team of fifty young Germans who, at the end of a day's labouring on the construction site, would wash, change and appear in the little village church to join the brothers for evening prayer. The church was inaugurated on the 6 August 1962, the Feast of the Transfiguration.

# Invitation to the Second Vatican Council

In the summer of 1962, Roger received a letter from Rome, from Cardinal Augustin Bea of the newly-created Secretariat for Christian Unity, inviting Roger and Max Thurian to be present at the Second Vatican Council as observers. On 10 October 1962, The Council opened in Rome. Roger and Max were present at virtually every moment of every session.

In times of obscurity, Roger admitted that he liked to call to mind Pope John XXIII's words, 'Be joyful, seek the best and let the sparrows chirp!' John XXIII died on 3 June 1963 and Paul VI was elected on 21 June.

## Pope Paul VI

Roger said of Paul VI:

> Paul VI was a profoundly good man, very close to the sanctity of Jesus Christ. He did not cut us off. Throughout his ministry he remained ever ready to listen.

Every year there were meetings between Paul VI and Roger. When Pope Paul flew to Bogotà in Colombia for the Eucharistic Congress (18–25 August 1968), he invited Roger to join him for the flight.

It was with some embarrassment that Roger recalled Paul VI appealing to him at the end of one audience: 'If you have the key to understanding young people, give it to me.' Paul VI gave Roger a beautiful chalice for the church at Taizé. This the community has kept, together with Pope John XXIII's breviary, which was given to Roger by John XXIII's secretary on the Pope's death.

## The Orthodox Churches

Strong links were forged with non-Roman Catholics invited to the Vatican Council, members of the Greek and Russian Orthodox Churches and, in particular, American Protestants, who were keen that Taizé should send brothers to the US. A number of links were also formed with South American bishops, the best known of whom, perhaps, was Dom Helder Camara of Recife, Brazil.

Among the most valued friendships was that which developed with Athenagoras, Patriarch of Constantinople. In 1962, Roger visited Constantinople (Istanbul) at the Patriarch's invitation. Athenagoras suggested that Roger should create an Orthodox Taizé. During a later visit to Istanbul in 1970, Athenagoras twice declared that for him Roger was a priest; that he would make his confession to the Prior of Taizé and receive from him the Body and Blood of Christ. 'The cup and the breaking of bread. Remember that is the only way,' were Athenagoras's last words to Roger.

## The community grows

The brothers themselves were increasing in numbers and, with the addition of members from The Netherlands, Germany, the US and Britain, the community was becoming ever more international. In 1969, a young Belgian doctor was the first Roman Catholic to enter the community. The first Roman Catholic priest to become a full brother of the community, Frère Marcel, had a special link with the region: he was born in a village nearby.

Since about 1970, the Sisters of St Andrew have had their community in a nearby village and have helped the brothers to welcome visitors who come from all over the world. They also help with the bimonthly *Letter from Taizé* and look after the young women who come and remain at Taizé for one, two or possibly three years.

## The Council of Youth

A Council of Youth took place at Easter 1974. Some 40,000 young people from every continent gathered for several days on the hill at Taizé to share their thirst for human justice and reconciliation. Because of the number of young Latin American bishops present at Taizé at the time, the celebration of *Pascua juvenil* spread like wildfire. There were subsequent celebrations in Latin America, North America, Asia and Africa.

## Marie-Louise

In 1975, Roger stayed for a while in Chile, a country stricken by a murderous coup d'état. In 1976, he spent a period of time in the slums of Calcutta, together with a number of brothers and a group of young people from four continents. The brothers stayed in a hovel in the slum where Mother Teresa had first begun her work. In the home for abandoned, parentless children

Roger came across a four-month-old baby girl. He was told that she would surely die because she would never have the strength to resist the diseases of India. Roger obtained permission to bring her to France. He had her christened Marie-Louise after his grandmother. For months, the little Indian girl lived in Roger's room, slept on his lap as he worked and retained extraordinary sensitivity to his voice. Gradually she recovered her strength. She subsequently lived with Roger's sister, Geneviève, and often accompanied Roger on his trips. She married and had a family of her own. Her name is now Marie-Louise Sonaly.

## Mother Teresa

Mother Teresa visited Taizé and, together with Roger, wrote prayers and letters giving voice to their shared concern for the suffering and the poverty, both material and spiritual, the 'areas of desert', in the Developing World and in the affluent West. In response to Mother Teresa's view that contemporary people need visible signs and references, Roger agreed to wear his habit everywhere. The white habit of the brothers is related to the significance it gives to Easter, for white is the colour of resurrection and joy.

## South China Sea

In 1977, Roger went, together with some brothers and an international team of young people, to share the living conditions of the poverty-stricken people living in junks in the South China Sea. In Hong Kong harbour they lived aboard an old houseboat and a hut mounted on stilts in cluttered, dirty water.

## 'Servant of communion'

Within the community itself, Roger did not want to be referred to as 'the prior', and, even outside, the word is used only in order to denote a function. The most recent modification to the Rule of Taizé substitutes 'servant of communion' for the word 'prior'. Roger no longer wore the cross he used to wear on his white habit as a mark of his office as prior.

## Prayer around the Cross

From young people in the countries of Eastern Europe came the idea of prayer around the cross each Friday evening at the same time in each country, as a way of keeping company with the risen Christ who suffers for those in tribulation throughout the world. Saturday evening celebrates the festival of the light of Christ, with the reading of the Gospel of the Resurrection and a prayer of vigil, which may last until the following morning. Sunday celebrates in a spirit of festival the risen Lord recognised in Scripture and in the breaking of bread, the Eucharist.

## The growth of the community

By 1985, the community of brothers numbered eighty in all. There were representatives of several different nations. There were several doctors and engineers, musicians, artists, brothers with expertise in agriculture, ceramics, computer science, sociology and theology. The community runs its own publishing house.

The Rule of Taizé was not seen by Roger as a Rule in the usual sense, but rather as a simple way of living a parable of communion. It is now known as the 'Sources of Taizé'. There is no formal novitiate period. It is a matter for the individual brother and for the community to decide when he is ready to be professed. There has never been any mention of obedience in the Rule. Instead, the community asks the brothers' acceptance that the pastoral task of continually recreating the communion of the whole be entrusted to one man, a 'servant of communion'.

In 1986, Pope John Paul II visited Taizé. More than 7,000 young people assembled in the Church of the Reconciliation. To mark the Pope's visit, the words he had spoken at the beginning of his ministry – 'Don't be afraid; open wide the doors to Christ' – had been engraved on the largest of the community's five bells.

## Taizé chants

When one thinks of Taizé, the chants are the first thing that come to mind. When an individual feels unable to pray, the shared chants and canons lead into a moment of silence where there is support. Those moments of silence in the presence of Christ might seem nothing, but with the continuity of the years, they touch the depth of the soul.

Roger said about the Taizé brothers:

> We are men awaiting God … Just live the day, just this day, and tomorrow we shall see.

There is a mystery about the moment we leave this earth. The life of eternity that lay ahead was something Roger felt people should not endeavour to define by their imaginations. For Roger, it was communion with God, with Christ and the Holy Spirit in whom love was fully realised.

## Death and funeral

During the evening prayer on Tuesday, 16 August 2005, in the midst of the crowd surrounding the community in the Church of the Reconciliation, a Romanian woman, Luminta Solcan, known to be mentally disturbed, stabbed Roger several times. He died a few moments later.

The funeral service was presided over by Cardinal Walter Kasper, President of the Pontifical Council for Promoting Christian Unity, and attended by religious leaders of the Orthodox, Roman Catholic, Protestant and Anglican Churches. Also present were representatives of the civil authorities of Germany, France and Romania. There were about 12,000 mourners.

## Brother Alois

In 1998, Roger had designated Brother Alois Löser (born 1954), a German, to succeed him as the person in charge of the community. Alois is a Roman Catholic. Though he studied theology, he is not a priest. He joined Taizé in 1974. Alois reminds us of Roger's consistent emphasis:

> Live in the present moment; simplicity; joy; mercy – these are the cornerstones of Taizé.

## Reflection

There is no hope for us to be bearers of peace if we are not, first and foremost, men and women of encounter, that encounter which takes place through the watches of the night and throughout our days with Jesus Christ.

We can find no other way to express our friendship than by listening ... Listen, and keep on listening, with a heart of flesh, in order to understand. Keep your emotions in check, not out of insensitivity, but in order to leave the other free.

# BIBLIOGRAPHY

## EDITH STEIN

*Edith Stein - Life in a Jewish Family 1891–1916*. An Autobiography. Translated by Jospehine Koeppel, OCD. ICS Publications, Washington, DC 1986.

Koeppel, Josephine, OCD, *Edith Stein – Philosopher and Mystic*. A Michael Glazier Book. The Liturgical Press, Collegeville, MN, 1990.

Mosley, Joanne, *Edith Stein – Woman of Prayer*, Gracewing, Leominster, 2004.

## DIETRICH BONHOEFFER

Bonhoeffer, Dietrich, *Life Together*, SCM Press Ltd, London, 1954.

Bonhoeffer, Dietrich, *Letters & Papers from Prison*. The Macmillan Company, New York, NY, 1972.

De Gruchy, John W., *The Cambridge Companion to Dietrich Bonhoeffer*. Cambridge University Press, Cambridge, 1999.

Marlé, René, *Bonhoeffer – The Man and his Work*. Translated by Rosemary Sheed, Geoffrey Chapman, London, 1988.

Metaxas, Eric, *Bonhoeffer – Pastor, Martyr, Prophet, Spy*. Thomas Nelson, Nashville, TN, 2010.

## POPE SAINT JOHN XXIII

Pope John XXIII, *Journal of a Soul*. Translated by Dorothy White. Geoffrey Chapman, London, 1964.

Hebblethwaite, Peter, *John XXIII – Pope of the Council*. Geoffrey Chapman, London, 1984.

*Pope John XXIII – Essential Writings*. Selected with an Introduction by Jean Maalouf. Modern Spiritual Master Series. Orbis Books, Maryknoll, NY, 2008.

Rosenberg, Randall S., *The Vision of Saint John XXIII*. Paulist Press, New York, NY/Mahwah, NJ, 2014.

## THOMAS MERTON

*Thomas Merton – A Life in Letters: The Essential Collection*. Edited by William H. Shannon and Christine M. Bochen. Harper Collins, NY, 2008.

Merton, Thomas, *The Seven Storey Mountain*, SPCK Classics, London, Centenary Edition 2015.

Pennington, M. Basil, *Thomas Merton – My Brother*. New City Press, New York, NY, 1996.

## PAUL VI

Hebblethwaite, Peter, *Paul VI – The First Modern Pope*. HarperCollins, London, 1993.

## DOROTHY DAY

*Dorothy Day – Selected Writings*. Edited and with an Introduction by Robert Ellsberg. Darton, Longman & Todd, London, 2005.

Hennessy, Kate, *Dorothy Day – The World will be Saved by Beauty*. Scribner, New York, NY, 2017.

## OSCAR ROMERO

Della Rocca, Robert Morozzo, *Oscar Romero – Prophet of Hope*, Darton, Longman & Todd, London, 2015.

*Archbishop Oscar Romero – A Shepherd's Diary*. Translated by Irene B. Hodgson, Cafod, London, 1993.

*Through the Year with Oscar Romero – Daily Meditations*. Translated by Irene B. Hodgson, Darton, Longman & Todd, London, 2006.

## PEDRO ARRUPE

Bishop, George, *Pedro Arrupe*, Gracewing, Leominster, 2007.

Burke, Kevin, *Pedro Arrupe – Essential Writings*, Orbis Books, Maryknoll, NY, 2004.

Lamet, Pedro Miguel, *Pedro Arrupe – Witness of the Twentieth Century, Prophet of the Twenty-First*. Institute of Jesuit Sources, Boston College, MA, 2020.

## TERESA OF CALCUTTA

Kolodiejchuk, Brian, M.C., *Mother Teresa – Come be my Light*, Rider, London, Sydney, Auckland, Johannesburg, 2008.

Mother Teresa, *No Greater Love*, New World Library, Novato, CA, 2001.

Spink, Kathryn, *Mother Teresa – An Authorised Biography*, (Revised and Updated) HarperCollins, New York, NY, 2011.

## ROGER OF TAIZÉ

Balado, J. L. G., *The Story of Taizé*, Mowbray, London and Oxford, 1981.

Brother Roger of Taizé, *Parable of Community*, Mowbray, London and Oxford, 1980.

Brother Roger of Taizé, *Living Today of God*, Mowbray, London and Oxford, 1980.

Brother Roger of Taizé, *Violent for Peace*, Mowbray, London and Oxford, 1981.

*Brother Roger of Taizé – Essential Writings*. Selected with an Introduction by Marcello Fidanzio, Orbis Books, Maryknoll, NY, 2006.

Spink Kathryn, *A Universal Heart – The Life and Vision of Brother Roger of Taizé*, SPCK, London 2015.